To my Darling, Wende

with all my

love forever.

POEM PORTRAITS OF INSPIRATION

BOOKS BY JAMES J. METCALFE

Poem Portraits of Inspiration
Garden in My Heart
Poem Portraits
More Poem Portraits
Poem Portraits of the Saints
My Rosary of Rhymes
Love Portraits
Daily Poem Portraits
Poems for Children

POEM PORTRAITS

OF

INSPIRATION

BY JAMES J. METCALFE

*

HANOVER HOUSE
GARDEN CITY, NEW YORK

FOREWORD

Millions of newspaper readers have been touched and strengthened by Jim Metcalfe's ability to express in poetry just what they themselves have felt or dreamed; many thousands more have found comfort and pleasure in his books. Now here is another collection, filled with new poems, but characterized by the same warm and perceptive approach to life.

These poems are not complicated and confusing; they do not express pessimism and depression. Instead they are simple affirmations of what is best in life. In everyday language Jim Metcalfe talks about everyday things, yet because this is poetry he adds a little something more—something which makes us recognize the feeling he expresses, yet know that we could never have said it so clearly or so well.

Jim has always written poetry but for many years it was only a diversion from a successful and action-packed life. At the University of Notre Dame and in law school at Loyola University in Chicago he won honors in oratory. Four years in the F.B.I. followed, and then nine years as an investigator for the United States Department of Agriculture. As a reporter and writer for the Chicago *Times* he won the National Headliners Club silver plaque for his undercover work in exposing the German and German-American Bunds.

Now, after living in Dallas for many years, Jim has moved with his family to California, near San Francisco. There he continues to write the poem PORTRAITS seen in over a hundred newspapers daily. Despite the danger and violence he has seen Jim believes, as he always has, in love and faith and compassion. And as we read his poems, we find that we believe in them too.

CONTENTS BY SUBJECT

HOME

Contents

Contents

Contents

THEATER

MISCELLANEOUS

POEM PORTRAITS OF INSPIRATION

DAWN AND DUSK

If you deny there is a God . . . Or if you walk in doubt . . .
Just let your eyes behold the skies . . . And take a look
about . . . Consider now the dawn and dusk . . . The bright-
ness of the day . . . And how the darkness settles when . . .
The sun has slipped away . . . Consider just these miracles . . .
The morning and the night . . . The fear in every shadow and
. . . The hope in every light . . . Oh, there are other miracles
. . . Including life and death . . . As earthly science cannot
find . . . The origin of breath . . . But just behold the chang-
ing sky . . . And ask yourself again . . . If there is not a God
Who is . . . The Ruler of all men.

HOW MANY FLOWERS?

How many are the flowers, dear . . . That I have given you . . .
As soft, endearing tokens of . . . My love forever true? . . .
Not just the kind that bloom in beds . . . Beside a garden wall
. . . Nor those that lift their faces from . . . The vases large or
small . . . But more importantly the kind . . . We cannot smell
or feel . . . And yet which somehow seem to be . . . More wonderful and real . . . The thank-you note, the look of pride . . .
The little word of praise . . . And other fragrant sentiments . . . For all your loving ways . . . Those are the flowers
of the heart . . . The ones that really count . . . And, oh, I
hope my each bouquet . . . Has held the full amount!

TROPHY

What does a trophy really mean? . . . What value does it
hold? . . . Is it the monetary worth . . . Of silver, bronze or
gold? . . . Is it a medal or a cup . . . For all the world to
see . . . As everlasting proof of your . . . Superiority? . . . No,
it is just a symbol of . . . Applause and heartfelt praise . . .
For effort that achieved success . . . In one of many ways . . .
It is appreciation and . . . A token of esteem . . . That by the
grace and strength of God . . . You did fulfill your dream . . .
A trophy is presented as . . . A public recognition . . . With
every hope that humbly you . . . Will further your ambition.

DREAM

A dream may be a memory . . . Of pleasant thoughts at night
. . . Or it may be a nightmare that . . . Is filled with growing
fright . . . It is the certain conscience that . . . We have inside
our head . . . That never seems to be awake . . . Until we go
to bed . . . A dream is soothing to our nerves . . . Or it disturbs
our rest . . . It is a fearful enemy . . . Or quite a welcome
guest . . . In either case, it represents . . . The way we think
each day . . . Our virtues or the wickedness . . . We try to hide
away . . . Sometimes it is a record of . . . Our every thought
and scheme . . . And then again we thank our God . . . That
it is just a dream.

BEST BLESSING

Of all the blessings I could ask . . . Almighty God to send . . .
The one I want the most is just . . . To have another friend
. . . To meet another person who . . . Is common on this earth
. . . And, like myself, is eager now . . . To prove his loyal
worth . . . I want to know my neighbors, as . . . I knock on
every door . . . And multiply my friendships to . . . The very
highest score . . . I want to multiply myself . . . In terms of
kindly deeds . . . To sacrifice for others and . . . To satisfy their
needs . . . To form another friendship true . . . With every
passing day . . . And help that soul to help itself . . . According
to God's way.

NO FEAR TOMORROW

Tomorrow holds no fear for me . . . Along my earthly way . . .
As long as I have tried to do . . . The best I could today . . . If
I have done each duty that . . . Was mine to undertake . . .
And lived each moment of my life . . . For someone else's sake
. . . My wealth is not important now . . . In dollars and in
cents . . . But only as my human heart . . . May prove its com-
petence . . . Because the world with all its gold . . . And all
its silver too . . . Cannot improve the character . . . Of anything I do . . . And so as I am honest and . . . I serve my
fellowman . . . I do not fear the future while . . . I do the
best I can.

ALL IN GOOD TIME

There is no problem on this earth . . . Too difficult to solve . . .
If we are really interested . . . And fervently resolve . . . There
may be many obstacles . . . And we may be afraid . . . But
God will give us courage and . . . The strength to make the
grade . . . If only we will bide our time . . . And wait another
day . . . And not be foolish in our hearts . . . And throw our
chance away . . . If we just think it over with . . . A patient
heart and true . . . And take our time in doing all . . . The
things we have to do . . . Yes, even faced with tragedy . . .
Or poverty or crime . . . If we repose our faith in God . . .
All things work out in time.

I LOVE YOUR EYES

I loved you from the moment when . . . I first beheld your
eyes . . . Those eyes that looked more wonderful . . . Than all
the starry skies . . . I told myself there could not be . . . Another one like you . . . And if you said you loved me, I . . .
Would be forever true . . . And so we came together and . . .
You gave your heart to me . . . And every happiness we share
. . . Is one more memory . . . Our problems have been numerous . . . And we have had our tears . . . But just a little
smile from you . . . Makes up for all the years . . . And all the
stormy weather that . . . Disturbs the passing skies . . . Can
never change my feeling when . . . I look into your eyes.

PLAY IT FAIR

There is no way to change the score . . . When any score is in . . . You lost by just that margin or . . . You had the strength to win . . . It matters not how hard you tried . . . With work and sacrifice . . . If you have lost the battle, you . . . Must pay the loser's price . . . But it is comforting to know . . . That you have done your share . . . And all throughout that contest great . . . You really played it fair . . . And that is most important as . . . You play the game of life . . . You must be honest as you face . . . The struggle and the strife . . . And only by your fairness will . . . You win the final fight . . . Because there is no compromise . . . Between the wrong and right.

BELIEVE MY HEART

A thousand different valentines . . . Are in the stores today . . . And yet no card is equal to . . . The words I want to say . . . I like the pretty flowers and . . . The picture of a heart . . . But nowhere is the message I . . . Would lovingly impart . . . I search the dictionary and . . . The poems old and new . . . But there is nothing to describe . . . The creature that is you . . . To tell my love, and thank you for . . . Your smile of sympathy . . . And all the other ways in which . . . You mean so much to me . . . And so I send this special thought . . . And hope to see some sign . . . That you will take my word for it . . . And be my valentine.

THAT CERTAIN FEVER

I look up at the lazy sky . . . I linger in the sun . . . And it is pleasant while it seems . . . That I get nothing done . . . I do not have the urge to work . . . I merely stroll along . . . Where all the world is standing still . . . And life is like a song . . . The air is filled with laughter from . . . The children at their play . . . And nothing seems to matter but . . . This moment of today . . . Tomorrow is so far away . . . It cannot ever be . . . And there is no concern or fear . . . To move or bother me . . . There is no moment of remorse . . . Or second to be sad . . . No doubt it is spring fever and . . . I guess I have it bad.

I BELIEVE IN GOD

One time I wondered to myself . . . Is there a God above? . . . A God of justice, mercy and . . . Of everlasting love? . . . And then I felt my human pulse . . . I took another breath . . . And tried to measure life on earth . . . Against that certain death . . . From where am I? Why am I here? . . . And where am I to end? . . . How could I be, except for God . . . Who surely is my Friend? . . . There is no other answer to . . . The theory of life . . . There must be One Whose Word allows . . . Our happiness and strife . . . And so I honor Him, my God . . . And thank Him every day . . . And humbly I implore His heart . . . To help me on my way.

NO PERFECT HOME

I envy not another home . . . However much it seems . . . The picture of perfection and . . . Fulfillment of all dreams . . . I know somewhere within those walls . . . There is a share of fear . . . And now and then as time goes by . . . There has to be a tear . . . There must be disappointment and . . . At least a small regret . . . And something that the occupants . . . Are trying to forget . . . Some house may show a brighter smile . . . Upon its friendly face . . . But there is never any home . . . That is the perfect place . . . And that is good for us because . . . How dull this life would be . . . With never any challenge to . . . Protect our family.

MY RAINBOW

I love you, darling, more than all . . . The rainbows in the sky . . . Because you are the rainbow that . . . Will never say good-by . . . That ties the clouds together and . . . That anchors them on earth . . . The rainbow that projects my dreams . . . To all that you are worth . . . I know its true beginning but . . . It seems to have no end . . . Because you are my treasured one . . . My everlasting friend . . . You are the only rainbow that . . . I ever want to see . . . As much as you are wonderful . . . And mean so much to me . . . I am not interested, my dear . . . In any pot of gold . . . I only want your love for me . . . To cherish and to hold.

ANOTHER DAY

O God, I thank You for this day . . . That I have lived on earth
. . . However poorly I have done . . . How little I am worth
. . . I thank You for the gift of life . . . The miracle of breath
. . . The healthy heart and lungs I need . . . To stay away from
death . . . I thank you for my friendships and . . . All pleasures
I have had . . . And for Your kindly comfort in . . . The
moments I was sad . . . I know that I do not deserve . . . Another day of life . . . As I am most unequal to . . . The struggle
and the strife . . . But give Your mercy unto me . . . Forgive
me for today . . . And each tomorrow I will strive . . . To live
a better way.

INSIDE YOUR HEART

Is it not how you comb your hair . . . Or how you wear your
clothes . . . Your perfect speech and manner or . . . Sophis-
ticated pose . . . It is the warmth inside your heart . . . The
sentiment sincere . . . In every kindly thought expressed . . .
That makes your friendship dear . . . No money and no flattery
. . . Can win affection true . . . The value of your name and
face . . . Depends at last on you . . . How well you serve your
neighbor and . . . The stranger on the street . . . In happiness
or sorrow and . . . In triumph or defeat . . . Your interest in
the welfare of . . . Another soul on earth . . . Reflects the
final measure of . . . Your more important worth.

MEMORIZING

There are so many things in life . . . That we could memorize
. . . If only we were interested . . . Without or with a prize
. . . It may not seem important but . . . A better memory . . .
Conceivably can bring about . . . Our greatest victory . . . In
daily business dealings, to . . . Improve upon the past . . . As
we have knowledge of the facts . . . And win our way at last
. . . And in our social meetings, as . . . We easily recall . . .
The names of people present at . . . A party—one and all . . .
But memorizing seems to be . . . Too much a mental cage . . .
Except for those who love it, as . . . They act upon the stage.

OUR STARS AND STRIPES

Our stars and stripes are more than just . . . A pretty flag today
. . . They symbolize the faith and strength . . . Of our great
U.S.A. . . . They are the banner that proclaims . . . The freedom of our land . . . With justice and equality . . . And
truth on every hand . . . From Tripoli to Tokyo . . . From
Yorktown to Berlin . . . Our standard has inspired us . . . To
lead the way and win . . . It is a flag made sacred by . . . The
blood of countless men . . . Who died for liberty and who . . .
Would do the same again . . . Let us protect our heritage
. . . With every firm endeavor . . . God bless Old Glory on this
day . . . Our stars and stripes forever.

TO LOVE AND BE LOVED

Our greatest happiness is that . . . We cherish and we yearn
. . . That we love people, and we hope . . . They love us in
return . . . To be a part of others and . . . To share the daily
weather . . . And in so many common ways . . . To live our
lives together . . . To ride to work and hurry home . . . When
time is running out . . . As Junior and his sister Sue . . . Are
gadding all about . . . To hear the ringing telephone . . . And
feel no longer haunted . . . By any loneliness, because . . . We
know that we are wanted . . . To love and to be loved by all
. . . Wherever they may be . . . And hold a place forever in
. . . Their fondest memory.

OUR COMMON WORRY

How many problems do you have? . . . How heavy do they
weigh? . . . How readily would you exchange . . . With someone else today? . . . If all our troubles could be placed . . .
Upon a common stand . . . Which ones would you be more
inclined . . . To take into your hand? . . . You probably would
choose your own . . . And grab them in a hurry . . . And at the
same time tell yourself . . . That you had less to worry . . .
You think that you have problems in . . . Some circumstance
or place . . . Until you see the hardships that . . . Your neighbors have to face . . . So just remember as you live . . . That
there are others too . . . And they may have much more to be
. . . Concerned about than you.

TIME TO RAIN

I like the rains in summer and . . . The ones that come in spring . . . Because they seem to brighten and . . . Give life to everything . . . But those that dampen autumn or . . . That wet the winter scene . . . Are not the ones to please my heart . . . Or make my life serene . . . The autumn rains are chilly and . . . Those days are never nice . . . While winter raindrops are the kind . . . That turn to snow or ice . . . The rains in spring and summer are . . . The soft and gentle kind . . . That everyone remembers but . . . That no one seems to mind . . . But when a sudden rain comes down . . . In winter or the fall . . . I do my best politely to . . . Accept its social call.

TIME FLIES

The longer as the days we live . . . The shorter every year . . . And by the fastness of our pace . . . Eternity draws near . . . When we are babies, life is slow . . . We suck our little thumbs . . . While just this moment matters, and . . . Tomorrow never comes . . . And then we start our childhood and . . . Tomorrow is a day . . . That does not bother us, and yet . . . Is not too far away . . . But after while the minutes run . . . The hours seem to fly . . . And calendars record the months . . . That suddenly slip by . . . And so as time is running and . . . No clock will ever wait . . . Let us pursue the way of God . . . Before it is too late.

SO MUCH I NEED YOU

How much am I in need of you . . . That life be not in vain?
. . . As much as crops and flowers need . . . The sunshine and
the rain . . . As every heart must have its beat . . . And every
lung its air . . . And babies cannot do without . . . A mother's
loving care . . . I am in need of you as much . . . As friendship
cannot live . . .Unless there is that willingness . . . To sacrifice
and give . . . As much as sails depend upon . . . The wind that
sweeps the sea . . . In all these ways and more, my love . . .
You mean so much to me . . . Without encouragement from
you . . . I could not ever thrive . . . Without your promise to
be true . . . I could not stay alive.

HAPPY SCHOOL DAYS

When summertime vacation starts . . . The children all pretend . . . They do not care for school, and they . . . Are glad to
see it end . . . But actually they miss it as . . . They go their
merry ways . . . And gradually grow tired of . . . The lazy
summer days . . . And they are really happy when . . . The
school bell rings once more . . . And all their friends are there
again . . . To greet them at the door . . . They love the black-
board and their books . . . The pencils and the pads . . . And
all the fond attention from . . . Their mothers and their dads
. . . Their hands and hearts rejoice in all . . . The things they
have to do . . . And while they would not let it known . . .
They love their teachers, too.

THAT BIRTHDAY GIFT

That birthday gift is just about . . . The nicest gift to get . . .
Because somebody kept in mind . . . The moment when you
met . . . Someone who took the trouble to . . . Record that
special date . . . When you were born, and never let . . . That
memory be late . . . However large or small the gift . . . It
signifies to you . . . That somebody along the way . . . Is faithful, kind and true . . . Not any relative, of course . . . No
cousin, far or near . . . But just that certain someone who . . .
Is equally as dear . . . That warm and hearty greeting and . . .
That special gift are meant . . . To praise you on your birthday
as . . . Your well-earned compliment.

OUR CHANCE IN LIFE

How heavy can the burdens grow . . . That are a part of life?
. . . How weary can the heart become . . . With struggle and
with strife? . . . Sometimes it seems impossible . . . To scale
the wall ahead . . . And there are lonely moments when . . .
We wish that we were dead . . . There is no purpose and no
joy . . . In anything we do . . . And we are prompted to believe . . . That we are really through . . . But why not take the
simple chance . . . That one more noble fight . . . Could conquer darkness and despair . . . With faith and hope and light?
. . . Why kill tomorrow's dream before . . . Tomorrow is
today? . . . Our greatest chance in life may be . . . The one
we throw away.

LET ME SUFFER

O God of Heaven and of earth . . . Behold my family . . .
Give them Your special blessing and . . . Be merciful to me
. . . Let not a single hair be harmed . . . Upon their loving
heads . . . Let not the sound of any storm . . . Disturb them
in their beds . . . Be with them all throughout the day . . .
Protect them when they sleep . . . And hold them in Your
loving care . . . As You would guard Your sheep . . . For they
are all I cherish and . . . They are so dear to me . . . That I
would suffer for their sins . . . In Your eternity . . . I know
their wrongs are nothing as . . . Compared to mine today . . .
And as I take the blame for them . . . Please wash their sins
away.

LET HEAL THE WOUND

The scab on any wound or sore . . . . A surgeon's stitch or such
. . . Is one we ought to leave alone . . . And never scratch or
touch . . . For it may open up the place . . . Where bleeding
can begin . . . And suddenly and dangerously . . . Infection
may set in . . . And so it is with friendship wounds . . . That
we attempt to heal . . . Misunderstandings and mistakes . . .
About the way we feel . . . When we have shaken hands and
when . . . Our hearts have said hello . . . Let us forget forever
all . . . The hate we used to know . . . Let us not pick a single
scab . . . Or touch a healing sore . . . Lest some infection start
and spread . . . Into another war.

MY LEAVES OF LIFE

I wander through the countryside . . . I gaze upon a tree . . .
And every colored leaf is like . . . A memory to me . . . I see
the golden summer and . . . The branches green in spring . . .
And every bough in wintertime . . . So bare of everything . . .
The leaves remind me of the days . . . And nights I used to
know . . . Including early childhood when . . . I first began to
grow . . . Each leaf becomes an older one . . . As time and tide
go by . . . And as it changes color, so . . . In many ways do I
. . . But when the autumn wind is wild . . . And leaves are
blown away . . . I realize that like any leaf . . . I have to die
some day.

WAITING FOR YOU

The stars are in the sky tonight . . . The moon is bright and
clear . . . And everything is wonderful . . . Except you are
not here . . . I know you have to be away . . . I know it has to
be . . . That I cannot embrace you and . . . You cannot talk to
me . . . But autumn turns to winter and . . . There has to be
a spring . . . And somewhere in this world there will . . .
Be time for everything . . . You will return to me the same . . .
As all the homing ships . . . And I shall hold you in my arms
. . . And kiss your loving lips . . . My heart is beating patiently
. . . My love is ever true . . . And all of me, my darling one
. . . Is waiting just for you.

LISTENING IN

When others use the telephone . . . It is a social sin . . . And
quite an underhanded act . . . For one to listen in . . . To pick
up an extension or . . . To stand behind the door . . . And
overhear a secret or . . . A small domestic war . . . To learn a
special business deal . . . A reprimand or squawk . . . The
gossip of a neighborhood . . . Or just some teen-age talk . . .
It is a base and sneaky act . . . To interfere at all . . . With
those who lift the telephone . . . To make or take a call . . .
The phone should be a channel of . . . The utmost privacy . . .
Except when G-Men tap the line . . . For our security.

KRISTINA'S GUEST

Among the pleasures that we know . . . Kristina to prefer . . .
Is having some young girl friend come . . . To spend the night
with her . . . They have a most exciting time . . . With supper
and a show . . . And then the television or . . . Perhaps the
radio . . . They get in their pajamas and . . . They jump upon
the beds . . . And whisper all the silly things . . . That fill their
little heads . . . Of course they go to sleep too late . . . As we
can see at dawn . . . When they sit down to breakfast and . . .
They rub their eyes and yawn . . . And when Kristina's slumber guest . . . Is back in her own home . . . We always find she
left behind . . . Her toothbrush or her comb.

NIGHT WITHOUT SLEEP

Sometimes we cannot close our eyes . . . When it is time to sleep . . . However tired we may be . . . And numerous the sheep . . . Our open eyes are weary with . . . The worries of our heart . . . Or we are overanxious for . . . Another day to start . . . We have to catch a plane or train . . . To keep a schedule tight . . . And just the thought of missing it . . . May keep us up all night . . . Our conscience may be bothered or . . . There may be someone dear . . . Who seems to be in trouble or . . . Whose death is very near . . . However weary we may be . . . Whatever pace we keep . . . Sometimes there is that hour when . . . When we cannot go to sleep.

OUR SUNDAY FUN

Yes, God is on the golf links and . . . Upon the tennis court . . . And in so many other ways . . . He is a real good sport . . . He lets us choose our favorite game . . . He wants us to have fun . . . But He reminds us that we have . . . A duty to be done . . . Our duty to remember Him . . . At least on Sunday morn . . . To thank Him for our life and for . . . The fact that we were born . . . To worship Him inside a church . . . Whichever be our choice . . . And beg of Him forgiveness while . . . We try to hear His voice . . . So let us rest on Sunday and . . . Relax in fullest measure . . . But let us honor God before . . . We start to have our pleasure.

IF WE WERE HONEST

How wonderful this world would be . . . With freedom from
all fear . . . If everyone were honest now . . . And everyone
sincere . . . If we acknowledged each mistake . . . And quickly
took the blame . . . Instead of trying to protect . . . A most unworthy name . . . There would not be a human mind . . .
Concerned with counting sheep . . . Or any conscience anywhere . . . That could not go to sleep . . . If only we were
honest and . . . We really told the truth . . . As much as we
were capable . . . When we still had our youth . . . How
peaceful and how pleasant life . . . Would be upon this earth
. . . If only we admitted now . . . How little we are worth.

AS CITIES GROW

Some people do not understand . . . That as a city grows . . .
There have to be some miseries . . . And residential woes . . .
There is no bus to make the rounds . . . The telephone must
wait . . . And telegrams, express and mail . . . May be a little
late . . . The sewer pipes are out of reach . . . The garbage
hauls are few . . . And there is little the police . . . And fire-
men can do . . . But everything on earth takes time . . . And
patient eyes can see . . . That every goal of better life . . . Is
reached eventually . . . And so the happy day will dawn . . .
When neighbors new will feel . . . That after all the city is
. . . Their castle warm and real.

PLEASE, FORGIVE

I know I hurt you many times . . . Throughout the years
gone by . . . Indeed I cannot count the days . . . And nights I
made you cry . . . But now I kneel before your feet . . . And
ask you to forgive . . . And grant me one more chance on earth
. . . To help your heart to live . . . I ask you, dearest, for the
hope . . . To try to make amends . . . For all the sorrow I have
caused . . . To you and all your friends . . . I realize now that
I was wrong . . . And I deserved the blame . . . And I am so
unworthy, dear . . . To ever share your name . . . But will
you please forgive me now . . . As much as I love you? . . .
And please accept this promise that . . . I will be ever true?

VICTORY IN DEFEAT

It's tough to lose a single game . . . Or even make a slip . . .
And it is tougher when you fail . . . To win the championship
. . . But do you ever ask yourself . . . When you have lost a
game . . . What brought about the final score . . . And who
deserved the blame? . . . There is no cause for crying when
. . . The tallies all are in . . . Especially if you have done . . .
Your very best to win . . . In your defeat you may have gained
. . . The greater victory . . . Of courage and of sportsmanship
. . . And teamwork loyalty . . . And as you go through life and
as . . . Success is what you make it . . . Your loss may be your
win because . . . You showed that you could take it.

WHY SAY GOOD-BY?

There is no need to say goodby . . . When we can say farewell
. . . And, after all, we may be back . . . In just a little spell
. . . Our destination may be far . . . And yet our hearts may
yearn . . . Until we cut our travel short . . . And suddenly return . . . In any case the word "farewell" . . . Is better than
"good-by" . . . Because it binds the friendly knot . . . That
makes a closer tie . . . It seems to sound a wistful note . . .
When parting with a friend . . . Whereas "good-by" would
draw a line . . . Where everything must end . . . So why not
say farewell today . . . Or whisper au revoir? . . . Tomorrow
we may want to hear . . . Some footsteps at our door.

THANKS, ST. PATRICK

St. Patrick never touched our shores . . . Along his holy way
. . . Yet many sons of Erin are . . . Our heroes of today . . .
The Murphys and O'Briens and . . . A wealth of other names
. . . So prominent in politics . . . In business and in games
. . . From labor to profession and . . . Success in all the arts
. . . The Irish of America . . . Have won our grateful hearts
. . . Their courage and accomplishments . . . Stand out so
much today . . . That Ireland seems to be a part . . . Of our
great U.S.A. . . . And so we thank St. Patrick for . . . The
noble part he played . . . By teaching them to honor God . . .
And never be afraid.

TIME TO EXERCISE

It's time to cut the grass again . . . And weed the beds and lawn . . . And in a dozen other ways . . . To exercise our brawn . . . Perhaps to paint the little house . . . And decorate inside . . . And sort of make a few repairs . . . To bolster up our pride . . . And if we are among the ones . . . Who live up in the North . . . It's time to clean the attic and . . . The basement, and so forth . . . It is not such an awful task . . . As it appears to be . . . It happens only once a year . . . And then our hands are free . . . Except for loading up the car . . . When we go on vacation . . . Or heaving coal and shoveling snow . . . When winter sweeps the nation.

LITTLE OR BIG

The little things that seemed so big . . . When we were very small . . . No longer are important as . . . We try to scale the wall . . . The problems of our childhood days . . . Have vanished from our vision . . . As now we are confronted by . . . Each weightier decision . . . The world is so much smaller now . . . With airlines overhead . . . And radio that picks up words . . . Wherever they are said . . . And yet our childhood memories . . . Are constantly beside us . . . As we believe in God and pray . . . That He will always guide us . . . And so as we are just a child . . . Or we grow very tall . . . We know that God, and God alone . . . Is Master over all.

ATHLETICS

Athletics are a blessing great . . . They give us exercise . . .
Along with friendly rivalry . . . In struggling for a prize . . .
Not only big events in which . . . The champions are crowned
. . . With cups or medals or with plaques . . . To make their
names renowned . . . But every contest that is held . . . If just
a private one . . . In which the only trophy is . . . The thrill
of having fun . . . Athletics are a classroom free . . . For
students everywhere . . . To learn the good of teamwork and
. . . The art of playing fair . . . To grow in character and
strength . . . And help us reach our goal . . . Of living right
with all our might . . . In body, mind and soul.

TO LOVE YOU MORE

I thought I loved you yesterday . . . And all the days before
. . . But now it seems, my dearest one . . . I love you even more
. . . It really could not be that way . . . Together or apart
. . . Because I always gave you all . . . The love within my
heart . . . But if my heart has grown in size . . . So has my
love for you . . . And that may be the reason why . . . I feel
the way I do . . . And if that does explain it, dear . . . Then I
can only say . . . You were responsible for it . . . In every
happy way . . . It merely means that you are now . . . More
charming than before . . . And you have helped my grateful
heart . . . To love you even more.

HOW DO YOU RATE?

How do you rate with all the folks . . . You meet from day to day? . . . Just what do you suppose they think . . . And go around and say? . . . What is your rating where you work . . . And in your neighborhood? . . . And is your grade at home just fair . . . Superior or good? . . . In other words, are you correct . . . And do you measure up . . . To every drop of credit that . . . Is poured into your cup? . . . Are you sincere, and does your dress . . . Of glory really fit . . . Or is your name synonymous . . . With thief or hypocrite? . . . What is the rating of your soul . . . Wherever you may plod . . . In spiritual and moral sense . . . How do you rate with God?

GOD LOVE YOU, SISTER

God love you for your kindness and . . . The patience you have shown . . . God love you for each suffering . . . When you are all alone . . . You live your every day for Him . . . In everything you do . . . And, oh, how many lives there are . . . Whose faith depends on you! . . . The little boys, the little girls . . . Each mother and each dad . . . And everyone whom you have helped . . . To smile and to be glad . . . And yet your loving sacrifice . . . Goes on from day to day . . . As you adore The Lord, our God . . . And live His holy way . . . God love you for your courage and . . . For every tear and ache . . . That you accept so willingly . . . For His beloved sake.

23

YOUNG TALENT

There is the young executive . . . Who seldom has his say . . .
But suddenly takes hold of things . . . To lead the only way
. . . Who startles all the others and . . . Who wakes them from
their dreams . . . And gives them new incentive with . . .
His merchandising schemes . . . He is the young executive
. . . With salesmanship in mind . . . The most important
salesman they . . . May ever hope to find . . . And as he makes
his business mark . . . He more than earns his praise . . . And
proves himself invaluable . . . With profit-making ways . . .
They better boost the bonus that . . . They have in mind to
give . . . Whoever have this special kind . . . Of young
executive.

PENCIL SHARPENER

Among my useful articles . . . I like that small machine . . .
That I have fastened to the wall . . . To keep my pencils keen
. . . The instrument I operate . . . To sharpen every lead . . .
That helps me to record the thoughts . . . That come into
my head . . . I merely turn the handle and . . . Each pencil
is like new . . . For smoother, clearer writing in . . . The task
I have to do . . . No knife can ever substitute . . . Nor gadget
take its place . . . And nothing else has anything . . . To catch
each cutting trace . . . I like the pencil sharpener . . . That
shaves in little bits . . . Indeed sometimes I think it helps . . .
To sharpen up my wits.

I PRAY FOR ME

I say this prayer for no one else . . . I say it just for me . . . And on the surface it may seem . . . I say it selfishly . . . But as my heart implores You, God . . . You know as well as I . . . There are so many ones for whom . . . I willingly would die . . . And so I say this prayer for me . . . To help me carry on . . . That through my efforts someone else . . . May reach a brighter dawn . . . That I may lift another soul . . . In sorrow or distress . . . And lead the lonely to a life . . . Of peace and happiness . . . I pray for me that I may be . . . Of service unto You . . . As I may help my neighbor in . . . The good that he would do.

THE PRIZE IS YOURS

I know how much you love me, and . . . Your heart is so polite . . . But, oh, I want to thank you for . . . Your compliment tonight . . . You did not have to say it, dear . . . It really was not true . . . Because you know our happiness . . . Belongs at last to you . . . You know that you inspired all . . . The progress I have made . . . Without your inspiration I . . . Would not have gained the grade . . . And yet you gave me credit for . . . Our measure of success . . . And led the whole wide world to think . . . I shaped our happiness . . . When all the while it was yourself . . . Who pushed and prompted me . . . To win this prize in token of . . . Our special victory.

NO TIME OFF

"Time Off" is relaxation that . . . So many of us take . . . If just to have the comfort of . . . Another "coffee-break" . . . We take time off from daily cares . . . As often as we may . . . And that is always good for us . . . Throughout the working day . . . But there is one exception as . . . We go along in life . . . We cannot have vacations from . . . Our moral stress and strife . . . We cannot take time off from God . . . From decency and good . . . Or from the obligations that . . . We owe our neighborhood . . . Our struggle for salvation is . . . An everlasting fight . . . And there can be no compromise . . . Between the wrong and right.

WHY NOT STAY HOME?

Your children are a problem when . . . They still are very small . . . Unless you have a sitter who . . . Will answer every call . . . It's good to get away from them . . . And go your merry way . . . With laughter and with dancing in . . . The moments made for play . . . But there are sitters of all kinds . . . And there are parents too . . . Who are a bit old-fashioned and . . . Who have a different view . . . Who would not leave their children for . . . A moment out of sight . . . But sacrifice their pleasure through . . . Each hour, day and night . . . The sitter may be marvelous . . . Courageous, good and strong . . . But who could fill the parents' place . . . If anything went wrong?

FRIEND WITHOUT END

I owe my faith in everything . . . To you, my dearest friend
. . . Because your friendship always was . . . And it will never
end . . . It always was, because it seems . . . Like countless
years ago . . . When first we walked as partners in . . . The
sunshine and the snow . . . And it will never reach its end
. . . As long as we may live . . . Because we share each other
and . . . We have so much to give . . . Your friendship is
eternal and . . . My faith is ever true . . . As you have given
me belief . . . In God and life and you . . . I thank you friend,
and every day . . . I say a fervent prayer . . . That God will
always bless you and . . . Protect you everywhere.

AT THE CAFETERIA

I like the cafeteria . . . I like to stand in line . . . To look at all
the children small . . . And wish that they were mine . . . The
babies in their fathers' arms . . . The youngsters at their feet
. . . While loving mothers choose with care . . . The vege-
tables and meat . . . I like to watch each baby in . . . Its high
chair at the table . . . Consuming food and chortling . . . As
much as it is able . . . And, oh, I love that precious smile . . .
Whenever I can see . . . Some baby girl who turns her head
. . . And seems to flirt with me . . . Oh, I would give a million
if . . . Those children all were mine . . . And I would stand
forever in . . . That cafeteria line.

MRS. DIPLOMAT

My wife is quite a diplomat . . . And good at playing games
. . . Especially when we get mad . . . And call each other
names . . . For if the doorbell interrupts . . . And visitors
come in . . . Her pouty mood has vanished and . . . She greets
them with a grin . . . And as we take our places and . . .
The conversation flows . . . She talks real sweet and smiles
at me . . . And no one ever knows . . . And nobody would ever
think . . . And nobody could tell . . . That I was in the dog-
house and . . . That things were not so well . . . But even
more I love her for . . . The way she carries on . . . In that
forgetful fashion when . . . The visitors are gone.

NO FAIRY TALE

If I could write a fairy tale . . . The hero would be you . . .
And when I finished it, I'd wish . . . That it would all come
true . . . That you would be Prince Charming who . . . Would
quickly rescue me . . . And free me from the prison of . . .
That castle by the sea . . . That you and I would ride in state
. . . With cheers and song and laughter . . . And we would
live in happiness . . . Today and ever after . . . But fairy tales
and story books . . . Can never quite come true . . . The same
as nothing sweet enough . . . Can be compared to you . . . I
love you as the lover who . . . Is really down to earth . . .
And in your arms and near your heart . . . I know your wondrous worth.

YOUR TIME TO SPARE

How many minutes of the day . . . Are those that you can
spare? . . . It all depends upon your heart . . . And if you really
care . . . You can seclude yourself at home . . . Or in your
business place . . . And there will be those people you . . .
Will never have to face . . . But actually you know you have
. . . The time to set aside . . . And you can hear their problems
and . . . Take care of them in stride . . . It is so easy to be kind
. . . By opening your heart . . . And God will bless your willingness . . . To do your gracious part . . . A little extra time
each day . . . A moment here and there . . . And you will be
rewarded for . . . The goodness that you share.

PUNCH AND JUDY

Punch and Judy is a show . . . All children like to see . . . It
stirs imagination for . . . The heroes they would be . . . Because in nine times out of ten . . . The devil loses out . . .
And in addition he receives . . . A most resounding clout . . .
It gives them inspiration and . . . Perhaps some courage too
. . . To carry out in their own way . . . The tasks they have to
do . . . But as they strive to emulate . . . May children never
be . . . As puppets that are pulled by strings . . . To shape their
destiny . . . May they be free from influence . . . As they
pursue their way . . . To help the whole wide world to reach
. . . A bright and better day.

How many hours in your home . . . Is God your welcome guest? . . . And do you treat Him just as well . . . Or better than the rest? . . . You need not serve Him food and drink . . . Or entertain him there . . . But only to remember Him . . . With now and then a prayer . . . To show Him that you love Him by . . . The way you love each other . . . Your wife, your husband—mother, dad . . . Your sister or your brother . . . Your virtues are His dinner and . . . Your prayer becomes His drink . . . And you can keep Him happy with . . . The kindly thoughts you think . . . If you respect and treat Him as . . . Your most important guest . . . He will be grateful, and your home . . . Will be forever blest.

WINTER SEA

The snow that falls this evening is . . . Of no concern to me . . . I sit before the fireplace . . . And dream of ships at sea . . . I dream of sailors in their blues . . . And fishermen with nets . . . And all the ripples and the waves . . . That nobody forgets . . . The boats that dare the ocean when . . . The weather flags say no . . . The cruisers and destroyers that . . . Defy the winds that blow . . . Of course they have their safety rules . . . But still they take their chance . . . And that is truly seamanship . . . And nautical romance . . . And as the snowflakes fall and as . . . The fire comforts me . . . I wish that I could leave my hearth . . . And join the men at sea.

MY LONELY DAY

I see you when we breakfast and . . . When dinnertime is here . . . And I am with you through the night . . . To comfort and to cheer . . . But, oh, those hours of the day . . . When we must be apart . . . Those hours, darling, when I long . . . To hold you to my heart! . . . I wish the day, as much as night . . . Belonged to you and me . . . That bread and butter, home and hearth . . . And luxuries were free . . . But if we were together, dear . . . Each moment of this life . . . And never had to face the least . . . Of struggle or of strife . . . We could not grow in character . . . Or ever prove our worth . . . No soul is made by God to have . . . Its paradise on earth.

SERIOUS PROBLEM

The problems of our children seem . . . So small to us today . . . Whereas if we were young again . . . It would not be that way . . . We have forgotten what it is . . . To be of early age . . . To lift the heavy book of life . . . And slowly turn each page . . . To grasp the meaning of this world . . . And grope our way around . . . To be dismayed, and yet to keep . . . Our feet upon the ground . . . If only we would help them now . . . As once we needed aid . . . To teach their hearts to understand . . . And never be afraid . . . Their problems are important and . . . They make a lot of sense . . . And we should help them all we can . . . With our experience.

BEAUTIFUL APRIL

April days are beautiful . . . In sunshine and in rain . . . Even for the wistful eyes . . . Behind the window-pane . . . Trees are turning green again . . . The earth begins to stir . . . And somewhere in the city park . . . A lover looks for her . . . Gentle breezes nudge the dreams . . . That wander in the air . . . Faith and courage fill the heart . . . And hope is everywhere . . . Joyful is the morning in . . . The song of chapel bells . . . Fragrant are the flowers and . . . The pungent kitchen smells . . . All the day is beautiful . . . And magic is the night . . . Gowned in golden moonlight, trimmed . . . With stars of silver bright.

FIRST TO CHURCH

Sunday is the day to dream . . . To rest and to relax . . . And put aside the working world . . . Of economic facts . . . To hide the family budget where . . . The tablecloth is spread . . . Enjoy the steak or chicken and . . . Forget the days ahead . . . But Sunday also is the day . . . Wherever we may plod . . . That we should take an hour off . . . And turn our thoughts to God . . . When we should give our gratitude . . . For all His gifts today . . . And promise to remember Him . . . In every faithful way . . . So let us go to church before . . . That chicken or that steak . . . And promise we will try to live . . . For His beloved sake.

HOW OFTEN, DEAR?

How often do I tell you, dear . . . I am in love with you? . . .
How often does the sun go down . . . Before a morning new?
. . . How often does the clock strike one . . . Or two or three
or four? . . . How often is there someone with . . . A message
at your door? . . . How many are the minutes and . . . The
seconds of each day? . . . How lasting is my loneliness . . .
When I must be away? . . . Propose a thousand questions,
dear . . . The answer is the same . . . The title of my song of
love . . . Is wound around your name . . . And though you may
not hear my voice . . . When we must be apart . . . My love
for you is constant as . . . The beating of my heart.

IF I COULD PLAY

The organ and piano are . . . Of nobler consequence . . .
Than just to challenge hand and heart . . . To great accomplishments . . . They are the instruments of love . . . Of hopes
and smiles and tears . . . And all the sentiments of life . . .
That wander down the years . . . If I could play piano now
. . . Or blend the organ keys . . . I could give voice in music
to . . . My dreams and memories . . . I could express my
thoughts in tones . . . That permeate the air . . . Yes, even to
the farthest sky . . . For God to hear my prayer . . . If I could
play piano or . . . Fulfill an organ role . . . I could reveal to all
the world . . . The longing in my soul.

33

ABANDONED BABY

How can a woman bear a child . . . And then abandon it?
. . . What greater sorrow can she cause . . . Or crime can
she commit? . . . The baby that she brought to life . . .
Through ignorance or shame . . . Or legally in poverty . . .
On which she puts the blame . . . There is no pardon for her
deed . . . And there is no excuse . . . That any infant on
this earth . . . Should suffer such abuse . . . Her flesh and
blood are in that child . . . As nature plays its part . . . And
all the love of motherhood . . . Should nestle in her heart . . .
There always is a way to solve . . . Each struggle and each
strife . . . With never any doorstep strange . . . To start a
baby's life.

I AM YOUR FRIEND

I promise you I am your friend . . . Whatever may befall . . .
I will be there to help you at . . . Your every beck and call
. . . You will be welcome always at . . . My fireside and table
. . . And I will serve your slightest wish . . . As much as I
am able . . . I will defend your character . . . Against the
smallest dart . . . With all the love and friendship that . . .
Are equal to my heart . . . No matter where your steps may
turn . . . How miserable the weather . . . At least in spirit
you and I . . . Will walk the path together . . . I will do
everything I can . . . To make your dreams come true . . .
Yes, I will even be prepared . . . To give my life for you.

O LORD, DELIVER ME

Deliver me, O Lord, from sin . . . Deliver me from shame
. . . Deliver me, O Lord, although . . . I know I am to blame
. . . Forgive the many ways in which . . . I trespass on Your
will . . . And with Your goodness and Your grace . . . My
humble heart instil . . . I do not mean to hurt You, Lord . . .
And make You suffer so . . . To lance Your side or bring about
. . . The heavy hammer's blow . . . I beg forgiveness for the
past . . . I promise You anew . . . That I will try to keep Your
word . . . As You would have me do . . . Deliver me, O Lord,
from sin . . . And help me to atone . . . That someday in
Your paradise . . . I may become Your own.

KEEP YOUR HEAD

The most important thing in life . . . Is just to keep your head
. . . No matter what the headlines scream . . . Or somebody
has said . . . Regardless of the crime reports . . . Or graft in
government . . . Or yet how widespread may appear . . . Sub-
versive sentiment . . . However common sin may be . . . However grave your plight . . . No wrong, however multiplied . . .
Can make a wrong a right . . . There is no way to weaken
now . . . There is no compromise . . . You must obey Your
God, to be . . . Accepted in His eyes . . . When all the world
is in a whirl . . . Be calm, be not misled . . . Remember you
are only clay . . . And try to keep your head.

NO MONOTONY

We may grow weary of our job . . . Or of our neighborhood
. . . But there is no monotony . . . In trying to be good . . .
We may get tired of some friends . . . Their all-too frequent
faces . . . And we may want to break away . . . From some
familiar places . . . But there is no monotony . . . In family
life each day . . . As we may visit church or park . . . According to God's way . . . We do not weary of this life . . . As
much as there is sameness . . . Indeed the word "routine" becomes . . . A challenge to our gameness . . . There can be no
monotony . . . When Heaven is our goal . . . As much as we
obey our God . . . And try to save our soul.

I BEG YOUR HEART

Tomorrow I will walk again . . . The streets I used to roam
. . . And I will hesitate before . . . The place you called your
home . . . That place so many years ago . . . That seemed
important then . . . But now is different, and could . . . Not
be the same again . . . And I will go inside the church . . .
Where once we knelt in prayer . . . And ask our God to keep
you in . . . His kind and loving care . . . And ask Him His
forgiveness and . . . Your own forgiveness too . . . For all the
thoughtless injuries . . . And wrongs I did to you . . . With
every step along the street . . . My heart and soul will cry . . .
That you will pray to God for me . . . The day I have to die.

SO MANY "IFS"

Sometimes a tragedy occurs . . . By just a twist of fate . . .
If something had not happened, it . . . Would not have been
too late . . . If someone had not turned this way . . . Or ever
spoken that . . . Or if the eye had known at once . . . What
it was looking at . . . There are so many "ifs" in life . . . For
all we might have done . . . We think that we were robbed
when we . . . Should normally have won . . . Sometimes it
makes us wonder what . . . This life is all about . . . And we
are very much confused . . . And ever so in doubt . . . Perhaps it is the will of God . . . There be a tragedy . . . And
maybe He decides against . . . The "ifs" for you and me.

BOWLING

Bowling is a game of skill . . . Where you deserve a crown
. . . If every time you roll the ball . . . You knock all ten pins
down . . . But bowling is much more than that . . . And more
than spares and strikes . . . It is a happy pastime that . . .
Most everybody likes . . . Good exercise and lots of fun . . .
It gathers friends together . . . No matter what the season and
. . . Regardless of the weather . . . You play it in an alley but
. . . A very different kind . . . From those that residences are
. . . Provided with behind . . . And there you will not be
condemned . . . By any nasty mutter . . . Or be disgraced if
you should slip . . . And roll into the gutter.

PAY FOR YOUR PAPER

I am a busy newsboy who . . . Has little time to spare . . . I
try to do the best I can . . . For neighbors everywhere . . .
I leave each paper on the porch . . . Or doorstep that I see . . .
And if the rain is coming down . . . I wrap it carefully . . . I
try to do the best I can . . . For all the folks who read . . . But
few of them appreciate . . . Or help me in my need . . . For
when I call on them to pay . . . The bill that now is due . . .
They offer some excuse or else . . . They disappear from view
. . . For every paper that I sell . . . I have to pay the price
. . . And those who try to stall me off . . . Are anything but
nice.

LIFE UNREHEARSED

Each play has its rehearsals, as . . . The actors learn their parts
. . . And strive for that perfection which . . . Will warm the
patrons' hearts . . . And that is fortunate for those . . . Who
walk upon the stage . . . In their endeavors to perform . . .
And act a certain age . . . But life itself is something else . . .
It is an instant play . . . With never one rehearsal for . . . The
things we do or say . . . Except that we can stop to think
. . . And so rehearse the mind . . . To keep the tongue from
speaking words . . . Untruthful or unkind . . . But otherwise
on sudden deeds . . . We have to stand or fall . . . And only
goodness unrehearsed . . . Deserves a curtain call.

HOW MANY LEFT?

How many friends have you today . . . Of all you used to know? . . . How many are the friendly smiles . . . That merely come and go? . . . Have you forgotten them, or have . . . Their hearts forgotten you? . . . How much did you receive from them? . . . What did you try to do? . . . A friendship is a partnership . . . And not a corporation . . . Where strangers make investments and . . . Expect some compensation . . . You have to do your equal part . . . To make the deal worth while . . . You have to share and sacrifice . . . With every passing mile . . . Consider now the friends you had . . . And those you have today . . . And ask yourself who is to blame . . . Along your friendly way.

WE KEEP OUR VOWS

When you and I were married, dear . . . My happy heart was sure . . . That our most sacred wedding vows . . . Forever would endure . . . And as the days and weeks go by . . . My faith is justified . . . As I am true, and always you . . . Are loyal at my side . . . Our promises remain intact . . . In all we do and say . . . We love each other, sweetheart, and . . . We honor and obey . . . There are some sudden moments when . . . Our tempers almost flare . . . But then the sea is calm again . . . As we kneel down in prayer . . . And so as God united us . . . He helps us stay together . . . No matter what the problem and . . . Regardless of the weather.

RECOGNITION

There is no nicer present we . . . Can give to anyone . . .
Than just appreciation for . . . A service that is done . . . A
little recognition for . . . The hours, day by day . . . Of loving
sacrifice to help . . . Some folks along their way . . . The gold
or silver medal or . . . The handsome parchment scroll . . .
That testifies eternally . . . To that unselfish role . . . It is be-
fitting in this life . . . That we extend our thanks . . . To
those who serve us privately . . . Or in our public ranks . . .
A little recognition is . . . A tonic to the soul . . . And it in-
spires others too . . . To reach a higher goal.

PRETZEL'S CONDUCT

Our Pretzel is a dachshund who . . . Is cute as he can be . . .
And he is quite the equal of . . . His perfect pedigree . . .
He does not heed the children as . . . They romp with him
each day . . . But he is quite obedient . . . To every word I
say . . . He knows I am the boss, and yet . . . He knows I
love him too . . . As long as he behaves himself . . . The way
he ought to do . . . Our Pretzel chews on sox and shirts . . .
Unless my hand is there . . . To spank him and to keep his
mouth . . . From anything we wear . . . I love him when he
eats and plays . . . And when he takes a nap . . . But when
he must be punished—well . . . I have to take the rap.

IN OUR HURRY

Sometimes we just ignore the dawn . . . Or carelessly forget
. . . And never look for sunny skies . . . Until the sun has
set . . . We hurry through our daily chores . . . And take no
time to wait . . . And many are the beauties that . . . We
try to find too late . . . We strive for earthly glory with . . .
Our utmost energy . . . And overlook the greater goal . . . Of
love and sympathy . . . The goal of peace and happiness
. . . That money cannot buy . . . Because the only price tag
is . . . How much we really try . . . How well we serve our
neighbor and . . . The stranger on the street . . . Such is the
final measure of . . . Our conquest or defeat.

WHAT RING IS THAT?

What is that ring you wear tonight? . . . What does it mean
to you? . . . Is it your vow to someone else . . . To be forever
true? . . . And if that is the truth, my dear . . . Why did you
keep this date . . . Instead of telling me at once . . . There
was no use to wait? . . . But let me take a closer look . . . As
now I clasp your hand . . . Forgive me, dear, for doubting you
. . . At last I understand . . . It is no pledge of love, it is . . .
Your own scholastic ring . . . Imbued with alma mater and
. . . The songs you used to sing . . . Oh, darling, draw your
hand aside . . . And keep your finger free . . . Until it wears
the wedding ring . . . That holds you close to me.

Our Camp Fire Girls devote themselves . . . To work and health and love . . . Especially in the great outdoors . . . With magic skies above . . . They share the sunshine and the rain . . . The mountains and the trees . . . The moon, the stars and all the joys . . . Of girlhood memories . . . This is their law—to worship God . . . Seek beauty on this earth . . . To render service and pursue . . . All knowledge truly worth . . . To be trustworthy and preserve . . . Their health in school and play . . . To glorify good effort and . . . Be happy every day . . . God bless our worthy Camp Fire Girls . . . As now we say our thanks . . . And shower glowing praises on . . . Their honors and their ranks.

THANK YOU, GOD

We thank You, God, for everything . . . That we possess to-day . . . Our happiness and comfort and . . . Our democratic way . . . The freedom of our country that . . . We struggle to defend . . . Against whatever enemy . . . That tyranny may end . . . We thank You for the turkey and . . . Delicious dressing too . . . And for our sweet potatoes we . . . Are grateful unto you . . . We thank You, God, for life on earth . . . And for security . . . As You have been The Guardian . . . Of every family . . . We thank You, God, with all our hearts . . . On This Thanksgiving Day . . . And with Your blessing may we live . . . According to Your way.

JUST AS YOU ARE

Do not apologize, my love . . . I want you as you are . . . No one is faultless on this earth . . . Or perfect as a star . . . You have your faults, and I have mine . . . As human beings do . . . And your confession does not change . . . My happy thoughts of you . . . We all have made mistakes in life . . . And we may make some more . . . However hard we try to guard . . . The seal on virtue's door . . . Whatever you and I have done . . . Let us forget the past . . . And let us join our hearts and souls . . . In union that will last . . . Forgive me for my smallest sin . . . As I forgive you now . . . And let us both begin anew . . . With our eternal vow.

A FRIENDLY NOTE

When you have nothing else to do . . . Sit down and write a letter . . . A cheerful note that probably . . . Will help someone feel better . . . Not in reply to mail received . . . Nor any words you owe . . . But just that friendly greeting as . . . Your pen begins to flow . . . Remember somebody with whom . . . You wish you were together . . . And tell him how you are and what . . . You think about the weather . . . Put in a little word of praise . . . A pat upon the back . . . And soon you will discover you . . . Have lightened your own pack . . . You do a gracious deed each time . . . You mail that kind of letter . . . And by that act of charity . . . You too will feel much better.

CIVIC DUTY

What is a civic duty, and . . . To whom does it belong? . . .
The contribution from a few? . . . No, that is very wrong . . .
It is an obligation on . . . The part of everyone . . . To strive
for each community . . . For progress and for fun . . . A civic
duty is a deed . . . That everyone should do . . . For nation
and for neighborhood . . . To see each project through . . .
If only at the ballot box . . . To register a vote . . . Or offer-
ing opinions new . . . In person or by note . . . A civic duty
is the means . . . By which we all pitch in . . . In happiness
or tragedy . . . To help each other win.

AGAINST THE STORM

The snow is falling steadily . . . The streets and lawns are
white . . . And soon the cars and buses will . . . Be anchored
for the night . . . It seems to be a winter storm . . . Though
winter is not due . . . But always there is weather strange . . .
That brings us something new . . . And in the mirror of this
storm . . . Our lives are well reflected . . . As we should always
be prepared . . . To face the unexpected . . . We should have
faith and courage now . . . To scale the highest wall . . . And
in the least emergency . . . To give our very all . . . So let us
get together now . . . And battle snow and sleet . . . And
prove once more our final score . . . Has never spelled defeat.

NO PERFECT CRIME

Suppose there were a perfect crime . . . And you committed it
. . . Do you believe that it would prove . . . Your cunning and
your wit? . . . Would you expect some glory from . . . The
evil you had done? . . . (You know, your name would have
to stay . . . Unknown to everyone) . . . How foolish can your
heart become? . . . Why should you waste the time . . . To
figure out and carry out . . . The almost perfect crime . . .
You might deceive the sheriff and . . . The neighborhood
police . . . And even fool the D.A. with . . . Your self-styled
masterpiece . . . But there can be no perfect crime . . . As
we are on this sod . . . Because whatever wrong we do . . . Is
always known to God.

I DO PROPOSE

You say you have no promise that . . . I will be always true
. . . You say I kissed your lips but I . . . Did not propose to
you . . . Indeed, I kissed your lips that night . . . But I was
speechless, dear . . . And if you said a word to me . . . I know
I could not hear . . . I could not speak, I could not hear . . .
Because I love you so . . . And you mean everything to me
. . . Wherever I may go . . . But if you want to hear me now
. . . I whisper to your heart . . . That you will be my own for
life . . . And we will never part . . . And, oh, I do propose to
you . . . Upon my bended knee . . . As now I pray to God
that you . . . Will give yourself to me.

HER DEADLINE

There are those deadlines every day . . . That editors must meet . . . But what about the ones for wives . . . When it is time to eat? . . . Their dusting and their cleaning they . . . May casually forget . . . But what excuse is worthy when . . . The table is not set? . . . Their breakfast deadline is the first . . . To satisfy each one . . . For husbands and for children as . . . They greet the morning sun . . . And then there is the lunch to keep . . . The youngsters on their feet . . . And deadline for the dinner when . . . The boss may come to eat . . . Those deadlines for the editors . . . And for reporters too . . . Are nothing quite compared to what . . . The loyal wife must do.

HIS WILL BE DONE

God does not ask your sacrifice . . . Beyond your strength to cope . . . He only wants your willingness . . . With all your faith and hope . . . He only wants you on His side . . . To spread His gospel true . . . That you will do to others as . . . You'd have them do to you . . . He begs you for your charity . . . The goods upon your shelf . . . To help your needy neighbor and . . . Forget about yourself . . . And every kindly act you do . . . Is one more candle lit . . . Before the throne of God where He . . . Will bless and cherish it . . . He is your God, Who does not care . . . How rich you are today . . . But only how you strive to live . . . According to His way.

Labor Day is time to play . . . For those who work all year
. . . And time for us to honor them . . . Salute them and to
cheer . . . In factory and mine and mill . . . They are the
real foundation . . . Of progress and prosperity . . . In our
beloved nation . . . They are the ramparts of our land . . .
In time of peace and war . . . As they equip the sentinels
. . . Who guard our every shore . . . They are the humble
people who . . . Are faithful to their labors . . . That we may
live more comfortably . . . And closer to our neighbors . . .
God bless our workers everywhere . . . And help them carry
on . . . Through every night of darkness to . . . A bright and
better dawn.

TO BE POLITE

The rules of etiquette are those . . . By which we are polite
. . . And strive to hold our temper when . . . We are inclined
to fight . . . The rules by which we say one thing . . . When
we intend another . . . Because our feelings are the kind . . .
Our conduct ought to cover . . . They guide us at the table
and . . . When folks are sipping tea . . . They are the constitution for . . . Our social policy . . . The rules of etiquette
are those . . . That are the public measure . . . Of how we
handle business deals . . . Or we indulge our pleasure . . .
They teach us to be kind and calm . . . As we believe is right
. . . And love our neighbors as ourselves . . . If just to be
polite.

AMBITION'S WEIGHT

Ambition can be wonderful . . . And it can be so bad . . . It can bring happiness, or it . . . Can make the spirit sad . . . It is reflected in the eyes . . . Of every human face . . . As it may strive to live in love . . . Or rule the human race . . . It can be for the good of all . . . Or just a chosen few . . . According to the measurement . . . Of what we want to do . . . Ambition cannot justify . . . The selfish little soul . . . That would destroy or injure to . . . Attain its final goal . . . But it can be the pathway to . . . The glory of success . . . As much as its fulfillment brings . . . True peace and happiness.

CANDLE SMOKE

I love the smell of candle smoke . . . When candlelights go out . . . It is a fragrance similar . . . To incense all about . . . It is a pungent odor and . . . Exotic as can be . . . That fills the room and wraps the world . . . In timeless memory . . . The common wick embraced by wax . . . A match to start the flame . . . And then a bit of human breath . . . To blow out all the blame . . . The candle conquers darkness and . . . It guides me on my way . . . And even when its brilliance dies . . . I do not go astray . . . Because I still can smell the smoke . . . And in my heart I know . . . There is the candle of my God . . . That will forever glow.

LEFTOVERS

Leftovers are not only foods . . . That rest upon the table . . .
When every guest has eaten all . . . He thinks that he was
able . . . Leftovers also can be those . . . That have a human
height . . . The ones who do not care, or lack . . . The grace
to say good night . . . Who linger on into the dawn . . . When
they should be departing . . . And probably were those who
came . . . Before the feast was starting . . . They are the ones
left over when . . . The rest have gone their way . . . And
there is barely time to sleep . . . Before another day . . . They
are the inconsiderate . . . Who look for lazy clover . . . And do
not mind at all the fact . . . That they were just left over.

MY CHILDISH WISH

I wish I had a sled today . . . To slide down all the hills . . .
Along the lanes of memory . . . To childhood joys and thrills
. . . I wish that I could change the clock . . . And start my
youth again . . . With everything as wonderful . . . And
innocent as then . . . As soft and white as all the snow . . .
That kissed the window-pane . . . When everything was beautiful . . . And nothing seemed in vain . . . I wish this were
a wonderland . . . For every girl and boy . . . Where everyone would live for God . . . And no one would destroy . . .
How happy all the earth would be . . . If nobody could fail
. . . How marvelous an ending to . . . The greatest fairy tale!

Help me, O God, to do your will . . . In all I undertake . . .
That every deed of mine may be . . . For Your beloved sake
. . . That I may spread Your gospel to . . . The corners of the
earth . . . If only by example, for . . . Whatever it is worth . . .
Help me, O God, to sin no more . . . In any shape or form
. . . But always to adore You with . . . A loving heart and
warm . . . From this day forth I want to serve . . . And strive
to make amends . . . For every wrong I may have done . . .
To strangers or to friends . . . Give me Your grace, and light
the way . . . To Your eternity . . . And if I stumble and I
fall . . . Be merciful to me.

TO START A BUSINESS

If you would start in business now . . . The rules are very
few . . . As your success depends upon . . . The simple things
you do . . . You sell a certain product or . . . A service people
need . . . And all you ever have to do . . . Is keep the mer-
chants' creed . . . To offer all your customers . . . A bargain
every day . . . According to their purchases . . . And what
they have to pay . . . The bargain need not be in cash . . .
Or in the quantity . . . The price may justify itself . . . In
terms of quality . . . Just sell your product honestly . . . To
anyone on earth . . . As much as you believe your time . . .
And energy are worth.

SHEET MUSIC

Sheet music is the printed form . . . Of tunes and melodies . . . To help the player's fingers find . . . The right piano keys . . . It is that code of lines and notes . . . And many symbols strange . . . That guides the voice to sing a song . . . According to its range . . . It is the magic means by which . . . All formal compositions . . . Are passed along on paper to . . . The singers and musicians . . . Sheet music is attractive too . . . With photos on the cover . . . The he or she you wish could be . . . Your one and only lover . . . And more than ever, as the years . . . Become a generation . . . That sheet of music gives your heart . . . A joyous palpitation.

SAFE IN THE ZOO

There never was a child on earth . . . Who did not like the zoo . . . The monkey and the elephant . . . Giraffe and kangaroo . . . The bear and zebra and the bird . . . With peacock feathers fair . . . Hyena and the tiger and . . . The lion in his lair . . . The zoo is most important to . . . Our adolescent age . . . But sometimes for us older folks . . . It turns a serious page . . . We have to fear the common snake . . . And all the bugs that bite . . . And there are certain animals . . . That fill our hearts with fright . . . Although inside the zoo there is . . . No panic and no flurry . . . The way those creatures all are kept . . . We never have to worry.

Tonight I write this letter, dear . . . To tell my humble story
. . . Including my confession and . . . The fact that I am
sorry . . . To let you know how little, dear . . . You were
appreciated . . . When we became acquainted and . . . The
seldom times we dated . . . I did not realize how you changed
. . . The color of the weather . . . And how much it could
mean to me . . . For us to be together . . . Perhaps this letter
is too late . . . For you to think it over . . . You may prefer
the honey from . . . A different kind of clover . . . But any-
time you change your mind . . . And life seems never-never
. . . I'll be your own to have and hold . . . Forever and forever.

ARROGANCE

Arrogance defeats itself . . . As any evil must . . . It is the
creature of conceit . . . That never can be just . . . It is the
haughty attitude . . . Of power bought with wealth . . . Or
other strength that is attained . . . By influence or stealth . . .
Some kings and queens, Napoleon . . . And Hitler at his
height . . . Are cold examples of the truth . . . That might
is never right . . . We cannot force our way through life . . .
Or covet all the earth . . . And win the smallest victory . . .
Of everlasting worth . . . Not arrogance but humbleness . . .
Will gain the goal we seek . . . As God will give the earth to
all . . . The gentle and the meek.

CAMPER KRIS

Last summer Kris went off to camp . . . And there she took a
course . . . In how to handle sailboats and . . . The way to ride
a horse . . . She also played some tennis and . . . She tried
out archery . . . And everything she undertook . . . She did
successfully . . . And now our Kris can hardly wait . . . For
summer skies of blue . . . With camping days and happy songs
. . . And all she wants to do . . . She loves the water and the
road . . . That seem to have no end . . . The sky, the trees,
and most of all . . . Each happy little friend . . . There still
are many weeks before . . . She finishes fifth grade . . . But
she is dreaming of that camp . . . And all her plans are made.

AS THERE IS HOPE

No victory was ever gained . . . No goal was ever won . . .
Without the hope that helped so much . . . To get the job
well done . . . For hope is our encouragement . . . In everything we do . . . It is the medicine we need . . . For every
effort new . . . Without a single hope on earth . . . We would
give up the fight . . . And life itself would soon become . . .
A sad and tragic plight . . . No matter what has happened and
. . . How much we may have lost . . . Our misery and suffering . . . And all the total cost . . . Today is opportunity . . .
Another chance to strive . . . And every chance, however
slim . . . Should keep our hope alive.

I SAID I LOVED YOU

Tonight I said I loved you and . . . I never would forget . . .
And all I hope, my darling, is . . . That you will not regret
. . . Because you said you loved me too . . . You gave your
heart to me . . . And promised you would be my own . . . As
long as we would be . . . I mean, my darling, that I hope . . .
You will be always glad . . . And nothing that is part of me
. . . Will ever make you sad . . . I want to live my life for you
. . . And give you everything . . . That honesty, fidelity . . .
And love can ever bring . . . Tonight I said I loved you and
. . . I said it with my heart . . . And by the grace of God, I
pray . . . That we shall never part.

PRAYER FOR RAIN

Give us, O God, a share of rain . . . To save the harvest field
. . . That we may gather from the earth . . . As much as it
may yield . . . Give us the water that we need . . . To quench
our thirst and cool . . . The arid atmosphere of home . . . The
city, farm and school . . . Let not our livestock languish now
. . . Let not our poultry die . . . Let not our feed and forage
fail . . . Beneath a torrid sky . . . For every drop of rain you
send . . . We offer you a tear . . . Of sorrow for our many sins
. . . And promises sincere . . . To live a better life for you . . .
And make a nobler gain . . . O God, please listen to our prayer
. . . And bless us with Your rain.

SANTA IS REAL

Of course there is a Santa Claus . . . Who comes at Christmas-
time . . . He is familiar to us all . . . In story-book and rhyme
. . . We cannot gaze into his eyes . . . Or watch him come and
go . . . No more than we can see the wind . . . Though we
can feel it blow . . . But Santa Claus is really true . . . For
every heart sincere . . . Because we feel him like the wind . . .
And know that he is here . . . He is the Christmas spirit in
. . . The Christian soul of man . . . To love his God and neighbor and . . . Give everything he can . . . Yes, Santa Claus is
each of us . . . As much as we endure . . . In peace with one
another and . . . Remember all the poor.

I LOVE MY FRIENDS

What could I do without my friends? . . . How would I live
today . . . Without their warm encouragement . . . Along my
weary way? . . . I would have no incentive to . . . Accomplish
anything . . . And there would be no purpose in . . . Whatever song I sing . . . And so my friends are life itself . . . As
they believe in me . . . And I am grateful for their love . . .
And for their sympathy . . . I only wish that I could be . . . Of
service in return . . . With some of all the happiness . . . For
which their hearts may yearn . . . But I am grateful unto God
. . . For all the friends I own . . . As in their kindly company
. . . I never feel alone.

DO YOU REMEMBER?

Do you remember long ago . . . The sunshine and the flowers?
. . . The secret of our happiness . . . In silent moonlit hours?
. . . The wistful touch of sweet delight . . . In every bashful
smile? . . . And how we wandered every block . . . As though
it were a mile? . . . As though we did not care about . . . What
leaves the wind would scatter . . . Because the world stood still
for us . . . And time could never matter? . . . Do you remember
in the park . . . When it was half-past nine . . . The night I
held you in my arms . . . And drew your lips to mine? . . .
Do you remember what we said . . . Without a whisper spoken?
. . . The promise that we promised, dear . . . Would never
once be broken?

WHY WORRY OTHERS?

Why bother other people with . . . Our problems in this life?
. . . When they must bear their equal share . . . Of struggle
and of strife? . . . Why add our worries to their own? . . . They
have enough to do . . . To shelter, feed and clothe themselves
. . . And seek horizons new . . . It is all right to ask advice
. . . When we are undecided . . . But as for desperation, well
. . . We ought to try to hide it . . . For when we pour our
troubles out . . . It really means that we . . . Are hoping for
our rescue through . . . Some act of charity . . . So let us have
the courage now . . . To strive for our success . . . The more
we do ourselves, the more . . . Will be our happiness.

HOW LARGE THE TIP?

What do you think should be the size . . . Of any tip you leave? . . . How much should be the present for . . . A service you receive? . . . In restaurant and in hotel . . . Aboard a train or ship . . . There is what generally is called . . . The customary tip . . . And yet there is no standard rate . . . By which you need abide . . . The sum of your gratuity . . . Is that which you decide . . . Some people tip because of fear . . . And some to play it smart . . . Some are too poor to give, and some . . . Lack kindness in their heart . . . And so the measurement is what . . . You can and want to give . . . To those who make it easier . . . For you and yours to live.

MY SECRET LETTERS

In every letter to your heart . . . I write between the lines . . . And just above my signature . . . I make my secret signs . . . Because I do not want the world . . . Or anyone to know . . . The special words I whisper, sweet . . . To say I love you so . . . I do not hide my love for you . . . By any moon or sun . . . Indeed I do declare it to . . . My friends and everyone . . . But there are certain messages . . . And sentiments so dear . . . That they are only for your eyes . . . And just your heart to hear . . . And so I hope, my darling, that . . . You read between the lines . . . And understand the characters . . . That are my secret signs.

FORGIVE US, GOD

Forgive us, God, for all the sins . . . That we commit today
. . . And help our hearts to understand . . . And live a better
way . . . Forgive us now the sins we do . . . As we are taught
to know . . . And those we may not learn about . . . Wherever we may go . . . We may be wrong in many ways . . .
We do not recognize . . . Because our hearts were never told
. . . And we are not that wise . . . We want to serve and honor
You . . . As fully as we can . . . And give the very best in us
. . . To help our fellowman . . . So please forgive us for the
faults . . . You find on every hand . . . And please excuse
our ignorance . . . As we misunderstand.

WHO HAS TWO JOBS

God bless the man who has two jobs . . . And labors day and
night . . . Because he's married and he has . . . A family in
sight . . . Because he knows that there will be . . . Another
mouth to feed . . . And he must meet the problem of . . .
Increased financial need . . . He is not thinking of himself
. . . But of his loving wife . . . And how to comfort her and
to . . . Protect another life . . . God bless the future father
who . . . Is working night and day . . . To carry on our family
. . . And democratic way . . . And may his seed be multiplied
. . . By generations good . . . To please our God and honor
Him . . . In every neighborhood.

FRATERNITY

What is real fraternity? . . . It is a group of men . . . Who
meet as faithful brothers and . . . Agree to meet again . . .
It is the close society . . . That naturally appeals . . . To those
who set their standards by . . . The highest of ideals . . .
Whatever secrets they may have . . . It is no secret now . . .
That striving for perfection is . . . A portion of their vow . . .
To honor God, to serve our flag . . . Protect the family . . .
And strive to be of service, each . . . In his community . . . The
real fraternity is one . . . Of deep fraternal love . . . That
every man is justly proud . . . To be a member of.

GOD BLESS YOUR DAY

God bless the day that you were wed . . . In love and sympathy
. . . And bless you more each time you have . . . An anniversary . . . As you abide together and . . . Remain forever
true . . . You live your happy married life . . . As He would
have you do . . . And as you bring some children forth . . .
A darling girl or boy . . . May every moment multiply . . .
The sweetness of your joy . . . God bless each sacrifice you
make . . . Each moment spent alone . . . And comfort you
as those among . . . The ones who are His own . . . God
bless you every day and night . . . And most especially . . .
When you embrace each other on . . . Your anniversary.

TO EACH HIS TASK

Each person has his task to do . . . However great or small
. . . A doctor or an office clerk . . . Whatever be his "call"
. . . The clergyman, the president . . . The ordinary wife . . .
Who feeds and helps her husband to . . . A better social life
. . . Each person has a special place . . . Whatever it may be
. . . To make a million dollars or . . . To raise a family . . .
God gives us certain talents and . . . There is no use to cry
. . . And wish for something bigger now . . . That seems to
pass us by . . . As long as we are honest and . . . We try to
do our best . . . God knows our needs and all we want . . .
And He will do the rest.

RETURN THE CALL

When people call you up, and you . . . Neglect to call them
back . . . Is that indifference or just . . . The memory you
lack? . . . Sometimes you promise to return . . . A ring that
you have had . . . Or in your absence someone writes . . .
A number on your pad . . . And when you fail to use the
phone . . . The caller wonders why . . . And it may be em-
barrassing . . . As hours wander by . . . If you are absent-
minded, then . . . You do have some excuse . . . But if you
mean your silence, you . . . Are guilty of abuse . . . You
may be bored or angry and . . . You may have cause to be
. . . But calling back is, after all . . . A common courtesy.

There are those happy hours that . . . We treasure with a friend . . . But by the ticking of the clock . . . There has to be an end . . . We wish those moments could endure . . . Forever and a day . . . Instead of melting into dreams . . . When time has slipped away . . . And yet there are the memories . . . That somehow never die . . . And constantly we cherish them . . . Although they make us sigh . . . And always we are hoping for . . . Another chance to meet . . . With conversation and a toast . . . And something good to eat . . . There is no better way to use . . . The leisure time we spend . . . Then just to share our pleasant thoughts . . . With some beloved friend.

MY GOD AND MY ALL

I love my spouse with all my heart . . . I love our children too . . . But more than unto them, my God . . . I owe my love to You . . . Because You gave them life, and You . . . Allowed my soul to live . . . And so I offer You my love . . . As much as I can give . . . Perhaps my selfish love for them . . . Appears to be so great . . . That my affection for You, God . . . Must be of lesser weight . . . And yet, my Lord and Master, how . . . Could I adore You less . . . When You have fashioned each of us . . . And all our happiness? . . . The heartfelt love I have for them . . . And all I think and do . . . Are just a small reflection of . . . The love I offer you.

HOW MUCH IS MONEY?

How much is money worth to you? . . . What does it really
buy? . . . A home, a car, your clothes and all . . . The things
for which you sigh? . . . Yes, maybe it provides for you . . .
The luxuries of life . . . And makes it easier to stand . . . The
struggle and the strife . . . But can it ever purchase those . . .
Possessions more worth while? . . . The love of those so dear
to you? . . . A friendship or a smile? . . . Can money bring
you peace of mind . . . When you have done a wrong? . . .
And can it change the bitterness . . . Of tears into a song? . . .
However rich or poor you are . . . This bell of truth will ring
. . . That no amount of wealth on earth . . . Can give you
everything.

I WANT JUST YOU

What makes the sky so blue today? . . . Why is the sun so
bright? . . . It is because last evening, dear . . . You kissed
my lips goodnight . . . You held me in your loving arms . . .
You promised me the moon . . . You said it could not be right
now . . . But it would be real soon . . . I do not doubt the
words you said . . . I know you are sincere . . . And that
is why my eyes behold . . . The sky so bright and clear . . .
I will be patient as the sprig . . . That only time can grow
. . . And all the while I wait for you . . . My heart will love
you so . . . But, darling, whether later on . . . Or whether it
be soon . . . I only long to hold your heart . . . I do not want
the moon.

THEIR SAFE RETURN

O God, I ask Your blessing and . . . Your special grace today
. . . That everyone will be all right . . . According to his
way . . . That there will be no tragedy . . . Upon the mountain trail . . . Or any life that may be lost . . . By any upset
sail . . . I pray that all Your creatures will . . . Be safe until
the dawn . . . Whatever they are doing and . . . Wherever
they have gone . . . Especially the ones who are . . . On their
vacation trips . . . That they will all be cautious now . . . And
make no foolish slips . . . Grant them the fullest measure of
. . . The joy for which they yearn . . . And then, O God, give
all of them . . . A safe and sound return.

YOUR GIVEN NAME

As you were growing up, did you . . . Dislike your given name?
. . . Or would your own selection then . . . Have been about
the same? . . . Your parents picked that name for you . . .
Because they liked its sound . . . And maybe too because it
was . . . A different one they found . . . Perhaps you liked
another one . . . Perhaps because you knew . . . Some boy
or girl whose character . . . And name appealed to you . . .
Of course you still can change it if . . . You want to go to court
. . . And call yourself most anything . . . However long or
short . . . But surely it is good to know . . . Your parents
thought it through . . . And had in mind your welfare when
. . . They gave that name to you.

MY FREEDOM FRIENDS

Whatever friends may comfort me . . . I want them to be true
. . . As much as there is loyalty . . . In red and white and blue
. . . I want them to be honest in . . . The country where we
live . . . With faith in God and government . . . And everything we give . . . I want them all to know and share . . .
The same philosophy . . . That everything belongs to God
. . . In each community . . . And only as their hearts believe
. . . And they are quite sincere . . . Is any blessing God bestows . . . So happy and so dear . . . I want my friends to be
the kind . . . Who always tip the scale . . . In favor of democracy . . . Where freedom cannot fail.

MERELY A METAPHOR

When I declare I worship you . . . And I adore you, dear
. . . I merely mean my love for you . . . Is perfectly sincere
. . . I do not mean I worship you . . . As I adore my God . . .
But only as a kindred soul . . . Created on this sod . . . Because
the only homage that . . . My heart could ever give . . .
Belongs forever unto Him . . . Who gave me breath to live
. . . I love my God above all else . . . He is The Only One
. . . Whom I adore and worship, dear . . . Around the moon
and sun . . . And so when I declare that I . . . Adore and
worship you . . . It merely is my earthly way . . . Of com-
plimenting you.

HUMMING

Humming is a musicale . . . Of rhythm and of rhyme . . .
Or it is just a mental mood . . . That seems to keep in time
. . . It is the artist, as he tries . . . An opera chord or two . . .
Or someone who remembers and . . . Is whispering to you
. . . Humming is the gentle song . . . That calms the wildest
sea . . . With all the beauty that belongs . . . To timeless
memory . . . But also humming is a way . . . Of music at
its best . . . As some young mother seeks to soothe . . . The
baby at her breast . . . It is that magic of the mouth . . . That
sings the human mind . . . It need not be the cultured voice
. . . But just the loving kind.

MY SQUEAKY CHAIR

My swivel chair annoys my wife . . . Because it always squeaks
. . . As she has been informing me . . . For many days and
weeks . . . She tells me that a drop of oil . . . Is all I need
to keep . . . My posture in condition, while . . . The family
can sleep . . . And still I occupy that chair . . . To talk to
everyone . . . And somehow as the hours pass . . . I get my
duty done . . . And still the squeak continues as . . . I move
my chair around . . . And constantly my wife complains . . .
About that awful sound . . . If I were not so lazy as . . . I
struggle and I toil . . . That swivel chair behind my desk
. . . Would get its drop of oil.

TO DO MY DEED

What can I do tomorrow that . . . I cannot do today? . . . And
what would be my poor excuse . . . For any such delay? . . .
Tomorrow may not ever come . . . Today is nearly gone . . .
Why should I be so lazy as . . . To let my spirit yawn? . . . I
know my duty and I know . . . That time is running out
. . . And there are those important tasks . . . That I should
be about . . . So let me mind my conscience and . . . Perform
each deed I owe . . . At least to keep my promises . . . Wherever I may go . . . Let me be faithful to each vow . . . And
every word I say . . . Forever in the future but . . . Especially
today.

OUR WORLD IS GOD'S

The universe belongs to God . . . And that includes our Earth
. . . With every form of life there is . . . Whatever be its worth
. . . The lion and the smallest flea . . . Each baby that is
born . . . The flowers in a garden and . . . The fields of
wheat and corn . . . Whatever living thing there is . . . Almighty God created . . . And only as it serves His will . . .
Can it be compensated . . . Our plants and fish and animals
. . . Have nothing now to fear . . . Because they have no
brain or voice . . . To show they are sincere . . . But we, as
human beings with . . . A will that is our own . . . Must
honor His commandments as . . . We bow before His throne.

WHY I CHOSE YOU

I chose you not as one of two . . . Or one of three or four
. . . But out of all the ones I met . . . A thousand souls or
more . . . I picked you out from all the rest . . . For in my
heart I knew . . . There could not be another one . . . As
wonderful as you . . . To me you were perfection or . . . As
near as that can be . . . Upon this earth and on this side . . .
Of God's eternity . . . Your warmth and understanding and
. . . The courage you possess . . . And how you seek unself-
ishly . . . To bring me happiness . . . I chose you for the fairness in . . . The way you play life's game . . . And if I had
another chance . . . My choice would be the same.

THE BASEBALL

The baseball is a little thing . . . That does not cost so much
. . . And for a million boys it has . . . That fond, familiar
touch . . . It may destroy a window on . . . Its hefty home
run mission . . . But it may also be the start . . . To big league
recognition . . . It often sails outside the park . . . When
major leaguers play . . . And how that ball is handled will . . .
Determine yearly pay . . . The baseball is an instrument . . .
That merely brings some pleasure . . . Or it becomes the test
by which . . . We take an athlete's measure . . . But whether
it is used for fun . . . Or in our search for fame . . . The baseball is America . . . And our historic game.

ACTORS ALL

We all are actors in our hearts . . . Whatever be our age . . .
As we appear in private roles . . . Or on the public stage . . .
In business and in social life . . . However brief the session
. . . We usually prepare ourselves . . . To make the best im-
pression . . . We may not practice every line . . . And move-
ment of the play . . . But we select our conduct, and . . . We
choose the words we say . . . We know our limitations, and
. . . Deceit is not intended . . . We simply use our skill as
far . . . As it can be extended . . . And as we smile, and as we
strive . . . To keep from looking tense . . . We all are actors
in our hearts . . . And in a special sense.

TAKES TIME

When "he" and "she" become as "we" . . . They start their
life together . . . And they are not concerned too much . . .
About tomorrow's weather . . . They want to take their chances
and . . . To make their way alone . . . And maybe that is
best for them . . . Until their minds have grown . . . There
will be clocks and calendars . . . To teach them many lessons
. . . Including all the ways in which . . . They ought to
make concessions . . . Today they are too young to know
. . . The problems they must face . . . As measured by the
hurdles that . . . Confront the human race . . . But gradually
they will find out . . . How many dreams are bubbles . . .
And if they keep on trying, they . . . Will overcome their
troubles.

I DREAM OF SUMMER

I know that it is winter and . . . The sky is overcast . . . But always I am dreaming of . . . The summer that is past . . . The winding roads, the hills and dales . . . The cooling ocean spray . . . The sunny skies and friendships new . . . Along a pleasant way . . . I like to see the snowflakes fall . . . And cover all the ground . . . And I enjoy the fireplace . . . With friendship all around . . . But summer seems to hold the edge . . . And I can hardly wait . . . Until the earth is green again . . . And travelers congregate . . . The lazy season of the year . . . By land and sea and sky . . . When hearts forget their troubles as . . . They let the world go by.

MY ONLY GARDEN

However beautiful are all . . . The flowers that are grown . . . Unless I dig the earth myself . . . They cannot be my own . . . I cannot claim the garden that . . . My neighbor has today . . . I have to plant and cultivate . . . According to my way . . . I cannot breathe the fragrance of . . . The blossom of success . . . Except as I have helped some heart . . . To find its happiness . . . Except as I have served my God . . . And given part of me . . . To smooth the path for those who live . . . In my community . . . I have no garden beautiful . . . With flowers soft and fair . . . Unless I walk in charity . . . For everyone to share.

THANK GOD YOU'RE MINE

I thought I gave you all my love . . . The moment that we met . . . That I could have no greater love . . . For anyone, and yet . . . Somehow I love you more and more . . . With every passing day . . . And always it grows stronger in . . . A new and sweeter way . . . Each second you are at my side . . . Your presence seems to bless . . . My heart and soul with faith and hope . . . And every happiness . . . And so perhaps, my only one . . . Your heart will understand . . . Why all my thanks and praise for you . . . Go out to all the land . . . I cherish you each moment and . . . I love you more each day . . . And thank our God that you are mine . . . In every prayer I say.

HOW TOLERANT?

How do you measure tolerance? . . . What does it mean to you? . . . How long can you withstand the deeds? . . . That certain people do? . . . What is the final limit as . . . Your patience may be tried? . . . And is there any compromise . . . To make you satisfied? . . . Or do you don a humble hat . . . And walk your way alone . . . And tell yourself that after all . . . To each belongs his own? . . . That ought to be the answer as . . . Your gentle heart endures . . . Because the choice is theirs, and so . . . The blame is never yours . . . Let others live as you would live . . . And never interfere . . . But should they seek your comfort, be . . . As kind as you are near.

MATCH

A match is such a little thing . . . Yet it can do so much . . .
Especially depending on . . . The surface it may touch
. . . The surface of the heart may bring . . . The flame of love's
desire . . . The tinderbox of politics . . . Can set the world on
fire . . . A match will light a cigaret . . . A pipe or a cigar . . .
Or fireworks that seem to soar . . . Beyond the farthest star
. . . It starts the stove or oven if . . . The pilot light should
falter . . . And softly it illuminates . . . Each candle on the
altar . . . And if electric power now . . . Should vanish in the
night . . . There still would be the little match . . . For
momentary light.

WHY RUN AWAY?

Did you ever have the feeling . . . That you'd like to run away
. . . And forget about your troubles . . . For your lifetime or a
day? . . . Did you ever try to do it? . . . Did you pack your bag
and run? . . . Did you get where you were going? . . . Did you
find that it was fun? . . . Or did you at last discover . . . That
there is no hiding-place . . . Where your troubles and your
worries . . . Do not stare you in the face? . . . Then perhaps
you learned the lesson . . . That your trials must be met . . .
And you cannot just ignore them . . . And pretend that you forget . . . For your problems will not leave you . . . If you try
to run away . . . There is no secure tomorrow . . . As it must
become today.

WITHIN MY POWER

I give you all the love in me . . . As much as I can hold . . .
And all my dreams of happiness . . . The future may unfold
. . . I offer you my everything . . . Tomorrow and today . . .
And all within my power, love . . . To help you on your way
. . . It matters not how high the hill . . . Or what may be the
price . . . Believe me, dear, I am prepared . . . For any sacrifice
. . . I want to share your troubles and . . . The storms that
sweep the sea . . . And in your darkest moment, dear . . . To
hold you close to me . . . I want to have you for myself . . .
And give myself to you . . . In every way that I can help . . .
To make your dreams come true.

SKID ROW

Somewhere in every city tall . . . Wherever we may go . . .
There is a certain section that . . . The people call, "Skid Row"
. . . It is that ugly urban sea . . . Of human derelicts . . . Who
have no aim in life and whom . . . No social law restricts . . .
The ghost ships that are drifting on . . . Through every day and
night . . . Without a captain of the soul . . . Or any port in
sight . . . Skid Row is like an ocean lost . . . Beyond the largest
map . . . Yet it is in the city and . . . It is a deadly trap . . . A
trap for those who give up hope . . . Who loaf and do not care
. . . Or ever try to be of help . . . To neighbors anywhere.

PRAYER FOR FISHERMEN

For all the fishermen on earth . . . I say this prayer today . . .
Be generous to them, O Lord . . . And help them on their way
. . . As once You talked to Peter and . . . He cast his humble
net . . . So may their daily catch become . . . As great as it can
get . . . But also in my prayer I ask . . . This miracle again . . .
That they not only search the sea . . . But try to fish for men
. . . To fish for souls to do Your will . . . And spread Your
gospel true . . . As Your disciples on this earth . . . To praise
and honor You . . . I pray that every fisherman . . . Wherever
he may be . . . Will turn his thoughts to You and to . . . The
Sea of Galilee.

FOREVER FRIEND

There is a friend who sometimes calls . . . Or has a card to send
. . . And then there is the one who is . . . Your real, forever
friend . . . Who thinks about you all the time . . . No matter
what the weather . . . Regardless of the miles between . . . Or
if you are together . . . Who does not let the days go by . . .
Until the weeks are old . . . And everything of memory . . .
Is somewhat strange and cold . . . There is the friend who cares
for you . . . As long as you are healthy . . . And there is reason
to believe . . . You are a little wealthy . . . But only one is
worthy from . . . Beginning to the end . . . Your everyday,
your every year . . . And your forever friend.

THANK GOD EACH YEAR

Each year on Constitution Day . . . Let us give thanks to God
. . . For one more year of equal rights . . . And freedom on this
sod . . . For justice, truth and brotherhood . . . In real democracy . . . As our United States have known . . . Throughout
our history . . . The liberty to worship and . . . To tell our
thoughts sincere . . . The freedom in security . . . From every
want and fear . . . Let us give thanks for every heart . . . That
lived and fought and died . . . For peace on earth and charity
. . . And progress, side by side . . . And let us ask almighty
God . . . To guide us on our way . . . That we may say this
prayer of thanks . . . Each Constitution Day.

IF I NEGLECT

If ever any day goes by . . . And I neglect to say . . . How
much I am in love with you . . . Forgive me, dear, I pray . . .
For it could happen only when . . . My mind is occupied . . .
With plans for all the joys for which . . . Your heart has ever
sighed . . . Each minute of the moving clock . . . While I am
still awake . . . Is one that I devote to thoughts . . . For your beloved sake . . . And even when I sleep, my dreams . . . However old or new . . . Are visions of the heaven in . . . My
happiness with you . . . And so if ever I neglect . . . To whisper in your ear . . . Forgive me and remember that . . . I
alway love you, dear.

TO SPREAD YOUR WORD

I am Your humble servant, God . . . But I am only one . . .
And on this earth I know there is . . . So much that must be
done . . . And that is why I ask you, God . . . For extra
strength today . . . In helping other souls to walk . . . According to Your way . . . To influence my neighbor and . . .
The stranger on the street . . . That more of us may serve You
now . . . Wherever we may meet . . . I want to be Your
messenger . . . As much as I can be . . . As much as I can
spread Your word . . . To all humanity . . . Give me that extra
strength, O God . . . And all the wisdom too . . . That will
enable me to be . . . A messenger for You.

LOOK NOT TO SIN

Strive now for knowledge that is good . . . In every earthly
way . . . As God intended for your soul . . . To live a better
day . . . But be not curious about . . . The strange and evil
side . . . Draw not the curtain from the cave . . . Where mys-
tery may hide . . . For as you delve into the dark . . . And
look behind that door . . . Your soul is very likely to . . . Be
tempted more and more . . . No virtue is mysterious . . . But
sin is always so . . . And there is that desire to . . . Discover
and to know . . . Behold the world that God has made . . .
With body and with soul . . . And in your gratitude to Him
. . . Let virtue be your goal.

Yes, even after all these years . . . If you would still be mine
. . . Your eyes would be as moonlight and . . . Your lips would
be as wine . . . My heart would span the years gone by . . .
And all that went between . . . Back to the days when you and
I . . . Were only seventeen . . . I never ceased to think of you
. . . When skies were gray or blue . . . Deep in my heart I
loved you, dear . . . And I belonged to you . . . I wish that
somewhere in this world . . . We two would meet again . . .
And somehow everything could be . . . The way that it was
then . . . But now I know not where you are . . . And only
God can say . . . If we can come together, dear . . . And
it can be that way.

OUR OLDER SONGS

Why is it that our favorite songs . . . Are those of long ago
. . . And they become more wonderful . . . The older that we
grow? . . . The melodies of modern times . . . Attract our ear
today . . . But as the calendar moves on . . . The music fades
away . . . The only answer is the fact . . . That we associate
. . . Each singing composition with . . . A very special date
. . . And every date of happiness . . . Is one that meets the
dawn . . . As love endures forever or . . . The sentiment is
gone . . . The older any song becomes . . . The sweeter it may
be . . . According to the picture of . . . Our heartfelt memory.

WHO DOES NOT GIVE

Of any wealth I have today . . . I treasure most my friends . . .
But I have no affection for . . . The person who pretends . . .
I have no use for anyone . . . Who hides behind a mask
. . . And who is not entitled to . . . The favor he may ask . . .
I will do anything for him . . . Who needs a helping hand . . .
But not for one whose plea for help . . . Is just a plain demand
. . . The one who very obviously . . . Is trying to impose . . .
And never has a sense of smell . . . Beyond his selfish nose . . .
I do not like the person who . . . Is greedy as he lives . . . Who
takes whatever he can get . . . But nothing ever gives.

TO SCHOOL AGAIN

It's time to dust the desks and chairs . . . Fill up the fountain
pen . . . The bell is ringing—it is time . . . To go to school
again . . . Vacation days are over now . . . And though we pine
and yearn . . . There are those books in front of us . . . And we
have much to learn . . . And only in the manner of . . . Our
formal education . . . May we expect to be of help . . . In
building up our nation . . . So let us join the classroom with
. . . The very best of cheer . . . And try to make much higher
grades . . . Then any other year . . . Let's buckle down and
study and . . . Get all our homework right . . . And prove to
every teacher that . . . We can be fairly bright.

WHAT MORE, MY LOVE?

What could I say to you that you . . . Do not already know?
. . . What secret could I keep from you . . . Or from the winds
that blow? . . . My heart is open unto you . . . As much as
every sky . . . I never could deceive you, dear . . . I could not
even try . . . You are the only one for me . . . As long as love
goes on . . . As long as night is beautiful . . . Before another
dawn . . . The whole wide world is quite aware . . . That I
belong to you . . . And so it must be conscious of . . . My promise to be true . . . What more can you request of me? . . .
What more is there to say? . . . Except that I adore you more
. . . With every passing day?

YOUR SERVANT, GOD

O God, I worship You today . . . I give myself to You . . . As
You have given me myself . . . And all that I may do . . . My
heart and body, mind and soul . . . And all I think and say . . .
Are only possible, O God . . . According to Your way . . . And
now I give them back to You . . . As humbly as I can . . . As
much as I may honor You . . . And serve my fellowman . . .
I am Your servant and Your slave . . . Wherever I may be
. . . And as You made me, I am Yours . . . For all eternity
. . . Give me Your love and lasting grace . . . On every hill
and shore . . . O God, forgive me for my sins . . . I ask for
nothing more.

THOMAS JEFFERSON

Thank God for Thomas Jefferson . . . So great in every way
. . . Whose birthday we Americans . . . Commemorate today
. . . He wrote the declaration that . . . Proclaimed our liberty
. . . And gave a life of service to . . . Our golden history . . .
As Governor and Congressman . . . And Minister to France
. . . He left no turning of events . . . To tide or circumstance
. . . The third man to be President . . . He served our country
well . . . With glorious accomplishments . . . Too numerous
to tell . . . But we remember him today . . . And every victory
won . . . And thank our God for one whose name . . . Was
Thomas Jefferson.

OUR DEDICATION

How many of us contemplate? . . . How many of us pause
. . . To dedicate a part of life . . . To some good, worthy
cause? . . . A little part of us each day . . . However small it
be . . . If just to help some stranger in . . . His human misery?
. . . We may not live as millionaires . . . And we may be quite
poor . . . But always there are others with . . . More troubles
to endure . . . Why not select some worthy cause . . . That
gratifies The Lord . . . And do as much as now and then . . .
We feel we can afford? . . . We need not underwrite a
debt . . . Or be a Santa Claus . . . But just to dedicate outselves
. . . To help a worthy cause.

YOU ARE SO NEAR

Whenever there is sunshine, dear . . . I know that you are
there . . . Whenever there is joy, I feel . . . Your presence in
the air . . . I seem to touch your spirit in . . . The golden moon
at night . . . And in the silver of the stars . . . So friendly and
so bright . . . Within the peaceful valley and . . . On top of
every hill . . . Where morning winds caress the grass . . . And
kiss the daffodil . . . Along the quiet avenue . . . Of garden
paths and gates . . . And on the passing calendar . . . Of sweet
and special dates . . . As in the white of winter with . . . Its
gently falling snow . . . I see a vision of your face . . . And, oh,
I love you so.

PARTY

A party is that pleasant time . . . When people get together
. . . To laugh and play and celebrate . . . Regardless of the
weather . . . When daily problems disappear . . . And fear
fades out of sight . . . The house is filled with song and joy
. . . And everything looks bright . . . A party is a pause in
life . . . To smile and get acquainted . . . And share ideas
on how the world . . . Should have its face repainted . . .
When folks delight in dancing and . . . They let their hair
come down . . . For all the gossip, new or old . . . To liven up
the town . . . It is that opportunity . . . For rudeness or de-
corum . . . Where usually the decent guests . . . Are those
who form the quorum.

ONE DAY WORTH WHILE

If I may live just one more day . . . To do a little good . . .
For all the world in which I live . . . Or just my neighborhood
. . . To help some creature on his way . . . To guide him
through the night . . . Until at last his eyes behold . . . The
Everlasting Light . . . Until he recognizes God . . . And bows
before His throne . . . And knows that now without His grace
. . . He must be all alone . . . Then I will say unto myself . . .
This day was worth my while . . . For I have won a soul to
God . . . And I have shaped a smile . . . And as I strive to serve
Him with . . . My efforts toward this goal . . . May God for-
give my errors and . . . Have mercy on my soul.

NO FRIEND FOR SALE

With money you can buy a car . . . And jewels without end
. . . A mansion filled with servants—but . . . You cannot buy
a friend . . . Oh, you can buy a human heart . . . To play the
friendship role . . . And probably that worthless one . . . Will
also sell his soul . . . But there can never be enough . . . Of
cash surrounding you . . . To purchase any friendship that
. . . Will be forever true . . . For honesty and faithfulness
. . . Are never up for sale . . . And all your wealth and influence . . . Can be of no avail . . . And you may try to fool
yourself . . . Or struggle to pretend . . . But finally you must
admit . . . You cannot buy a friend.

YOUR RING AND MINE

You gave a wedding ring to me. . . And I gave one to you . . .
And each became a circle of . . . Our love forever true . . .
Like any circle, they have no . . . Beginning or an end . . .
And that is why I tell myself . . . Our hearts will surely blend
. . . That you will always cherish me . . . As I adore you so
. . . And we will hold each other close . . . However winds may
blow . . . The circle on your finger is . . . The ring around my
heart . . . And mine is there to promise, dear . . . That we
will never part . . . And as the circles of our rings . . . Are
dear to you and me . . . So we shall be together, love . . .
For all eternity.

SUNDAY IN TOWN

Sunday is a silent day . . . Especially at dawn . . . When
buildings loom against the sky . . . And everyone is gone . . .
There is no sound on pavement and . . . No echo in the park
. . . All life is like a shadow in . . . The disappearing dark
. . . The atmosphere is one that wears . . . A penitential
dress . . . For Saturday and every day . . . Of sin and careless-
ness . . . Until the steeple bells ring out . . . And people
start to stir . . . And they remember now that God . . . Forgives
the souls that err . . . And then the city comes to life . . .
And God becomes a part . . . Of all who seek the blessing of
. . . His peace inside their heart.

NO HARM IN GRIPING

We gripe about our business or . . . We gripe about our pay
. . . Our transportation problems or . . . The weather of the
day . . . We gripe about the prices of . . . The merchandise
we buy . . . Our teachers and our homework, or . . . That
taxes are too high . . . But what is wrong with griping, as . . .
We go along in life? . . . It is a normal practice in . . . Our
struggle and our strife . . . It merely is our mouthy way . . . Of
letting off some steam . . . While we are busy working for . . .
The goal of every dream . . . There is no harm in griping if
. . . We still perform our part . . . And if there is no meanness
and . . . No hatred in our heart.

GIRL AND HER DOG

So many stories have been told . . . About a boy and dog . . .
About their close companionship . . . In sunshine, rain or fog
. . . And that is well, but now and then . . . Does it occur to
you . . . That little girls have dogs for pets . . . And they adore
them too? . . . We have a precious dachshund that . . . Belongs to daughter Kris . . . He always snuggles up to her . . .
And loves to get a kiss . . . He follows her around the house
. . . And out into the street . . . And when she hurries home
from school . . . They are the first to meet . . . Regardless of
the stories told . . . Or pictures you may see . . . In friendship
with a dog, the boys . . . Have no monopoly.

83

ALL PRAISE TO YOU

Whatever glory may attach . . . To anything I do . . . Whatever credit I receive . . . It all belongs to you . . . Because you do much more for me . . . Than ever I expect . . . And as you love and honor me . . . You build my self-respect . . . It is your inspiration, love . . . Your confidence in me . . . That gives me strength and courage to . . . Achieve each victory . . . And when you meet with others and . . . You speak of me with pride . . . I know how loyally you are . . . The partner at my side . . . And that is why I thank you, love . . . For everything I do . . . And for each conquest, great or small . . . I pass the praise to you.

OUR MENTAL PHOTO

No film can show as clearly now . . . Some scenes we left behind . . . As those enduring memories . . . Are mirrored in our mind . . . As we can picture certain things . . . That took our breath away . . . And that are just as real as if . . . They happened yesterday . . . We need not even close our eyes . . . To re-create that past . . . Because our heartfelt memories . . . Are pictures that will last . . . We see a new-born baby or . . . An empty bed at night . . . We join the laughter of a crowd . . . Or we are filled with fright . . . No camera can reproduce . . . The action that we knew . . . And match our mental image of . . . The photo that is true.

NEW YEAR FOR US

The calendar is turning and . . . Another year is here . . . And
I would tell you once again . . . How much it means, my dear
. . . How much it means to me to start . . . Another year with
you . . . My only one, so wonderful . . . So noble and so true
. . . I do not measure you in terms . . . Of seasons or of flowers
. . . I only want to capture now . . . Each moment that is ours
. . . But when another year goes by . . . It does remind my
heart . . . That we are still together and . . . Have never been
apart . . . And it is time to thank you, dear . . . For all the
pages old . . . Of calendars with all the love . . . That only
we can hold.

AS MUCH AS I CAN

I wish that I could bring some joy . . . To everyone today . . .
At least a friendly greeting to . . . The souls that pass my way
. . . I want to help them if I can . . . In what they strive to
do . . . As much as I am one of them . . . And I need courage
too . . . I never start an argument . . . Nor welcome any fight
. . . I only hope that somebody . . . Will know the wrong
from right . . . I long to be of service to . . . My fellowman on
earth . . . And make whatever sacrifice . . . My humble heart
is worth . . . I want to serve my neighbors and . . . To heed
their every call . . . But, oh, I hope they understand . . . I
cannot please them all.

SPRING TRAINING

Spring training days are here again . . . The wind-up and the throw . . . The horsehide hurling through the air . . . The batter's heavy blow . . . It won't be very long until . . . The stands are overflowing . . . With baseball fans from everywhere . . . Who boo or do their crowing . . . And that is our America . . . And our democracy . . . Where one may argue in defeat . . . Or smile in victory . . . Because our baseball represents . . . Our human way of living . . . Of playing square and asking less . . . Than ever we are giving . . . There ought to be spring training now . . . For everyone on earth . . . To put us in condition and . . . To help us prove our worth.

THANK GOD FOR YOU

Thank God for all the things in life . . . That I cannot forget . . . Beginning with the moment, dear . . . When you and I first met . . . The bashful gaze you gave me in . . . The moonlight of that night . . . And as I touched your hand I knew . . . That it was love at sight . . . Our romance and our wedding and . . . Our days and months and years . . . With progress over problems and . . . The smiles that smothered tears . . . The babies in their cradles and . . . The youngsters in their teens . . . And all the fullness of this life . . . A family truly means . . . Thank God for every memory . . . Of what we tried to do . . . Thank God for all His blessings and . . . Especially for you.

MIRACLES ARE

I do believe in miracles . . . They happen every day . . . No matter what some people think . . . Or any sages say . . . A life is saved from fire or . . . A hurricane or flood . . . Or by the quick donation of . . . The proper type of blood . . . A lifeboat is discovered on . . . The No-Man's Land at sea . . . Or some petition for divorce . . . Unites a family . . . A miracle is something in . . . An unexpected way . . . That changes the complexion of . . . A dark or dreary day . . . It is God's love for us—His love . . . That sometimes intervenes . . . To spare our undeserving souls . . . The tears of tragic scenes.

COMFORT OF HOME

What makes the comfort of a home? . . . The walls, the rugs, the chairs? . . . The basement or the attic or . . . The cozy, winding stairs? . . . Is it the bedroom, living room . . . The den or kitchen sink? . . . No it is not these things but just . . . The way that people think . . . The comfort of a home depends . . . Upon the heart and mind . . . Of occupant and visitor . . . According to his kind . . . As there is restlessness in life . . . And tendency to roam . . . So there will be uncertainty . . . And no established home . . . But as the lips of friendship kiss . . . And hearts are warm inside . . . We find the comfort of a home . . . Wherever we abide.

WHAT OTHER WORDS?

I am in love with you as much . . . As I will ever be . . . And
that is for as long as life . . . And all eternity . . . As long as
there are days and nights . . . With suns that rise and set . . .
And moons and stars that take away . . . The tears we would
forget . . . As far as all the rivers run . . . And oceans disappear . . . And there are mountains far away . . . That seem so
very near . . . As much as heart and soul and mind . . . Can
give my love to you . . . And my poor tongue can utter now
. . . My promise to be true . . . I am in love with you as much
. . . As God will let me be . . . What other words can tell
you, dear . . . How much you mean to me?

DIARY

The diary is any book . . . In which our pen records . . .
A history of losses or . . . Our progress and rewards . . .
It may pertain to business and . . . To some important date
. . . When we were most successful or . . . The offer came too
late . . . Or it may be the book of love . . . Where secrets hide
away . . . Until we are agreed upon . . . The thoughts and
words we say . . . It may acquit the innocent . . . Who stand
before the bar . . . Or help convict the criminals . . . As guilty
as they are . . . In any case, the diary . . . Is useful as can be
. . . As much as now it supplements . . . The human memory.

I PRAY FOR THEM

I pray for all my fellowmen . . . That they will pray for me . . .
And through their prayers I may be safe . . . In God's eternity
. . . I pray that I may serve them in . . . My poor and humble
way . . . And all of us will honor God . . . By all we do and
say . . . I seek no recognition now . . . Or any kind of fame
. . . I do not want a medal or . . . A ribbon with my name . . .
I want to be a neighbor in . . . The best way that I know . . .
And give my utmost to the world . . . Wherever I may go . . .
I pray for strength to do my part . . . While I am on this earth
. . . And may God bless my efforts for . . . Whatever they
are worth.

THE SKY

How little we appreciate . . . The marvel of the sky . . . The
peaceful blue, the dismal gray . . . The clouds that wander
by! . . . The clouds of fleecy white and those . . . Like mountains overhead . . . And clouds that funnel into black . . .
And never count the dead . . . We read reports on weather and
. . . We go along our way . . . And seldom bother to observe
. . . The sky we have today . . . And yet the sky is always
there . . . With moon and stars at night . . . And sunshine in
the morning if . . . God will allow that light . . . We ought
to look up at the sky . . . With less complacency . . . As now
it would remind us all . . . Of God's eternity.

EXTRA SPECIAL

There are some special things in life . . . That mean so very much . . . And then there are the ones that have . . . The extra special touch . . . That certain something just beyond . . . The special that we know . . . Above what we expect or hope . . . Wherever we may go . . . A present or a greeting card . . . A favor or a friend . . . Or loving lips that seal a troth . . . Forever without end . . . Those things that not uncommonly . . . Will play a special part . . . But now and then are extra good . . . And happy for the heart . . . And when they have that "extra," they . . . Are extra special sweet . . . And we are extra grateful for . . . That extra special treat.

YOUR STARRY EYES

Not all the stars of silver bright . . . Are gleaming in the skies . . . Indeed the two most beautiful . . . Are shining from your eyes . . . They are the stars that light my path . . . Not only through the night . . . But even when the dawn is here . . . With all its golden light . . . Two stars that guide me on my way . . . Wherever I may be . . . The one of love, the other of . . . Your boundless faith in me . . . And that is why I never fail . . . In anything I do . . . Because the stars for which I reach . . . Are really part of you . . . They are your eyes of sympathy . . . That help me reach my goal . . . And in the promise of your love . . . They hold my heart and soul.

SPRINKLER SYSTEM

We have a sprinkler system now . . . That waters all the lawn . . . And all we ever have to do . . . Is turn a button on . . . It is a bit expensive but . . . Is really worth each cent . . . Considering the energy . . . That formerly was spent . . . The garden hose is useful and . . . It drenches everywhere . . . Yet someone has to lay it down . . . And haul it here and there . . . And as I studied this, I felt . . . So sorry for my wife . . . That I decided to increase . . . Her luxuries in life . . . And now she has no problem with . . . Our bushes and our lawn . . . Which leaves more time for other tasks . . . She can be working on.

MY FRIENDSHIP VOW

I vow to be a friend to him . . . Who is a friend to me . . . My fundamental creed in life . . . Is that of loyalty . . . As much as he is faithful now . . . So long will I be true . . . In every message to his heart . . . And all I try to do . . . But if he ever lets me down . . . Or damages my name . . . The feeling that I had for him . . . Will never be the same . . . And yet I will not seek revenge . . . In any shape or way . . . By any act unfair or fair . . . Or anything I say . . . Although his heart may not repent . . . Before his life grows dim . . . I still will do the best I can . . . To help and comfort him.

BE CLEAN INSIDE

You take a bath and feel like new . . . With pleasure and with
pride . . . The mirror shows a healthy glow . . . But are you
clean inside? . . . Yes, you can scrub away the dirt . . . And
all the outward grime . . . And wash it off again, as it . . . Appears from time to time . . . But what about the inner bath
. . . You need to reach your goal? . . . The shower of forgiveness for . . . The sins upon your soul? . . . Your skin may be
as dirty and . . . As dark as it can be . . . But that is not important now . . . In God's eternity . . . For your external picture is . . . No evidence or guide . . . God only wants to know
each day . . . How clean you are inside.

YOUR NEWSPAPER

What is your newspaper today? . . . What does it mean to you?
. . . It is the messenger of truth . . . In all the news that's new
. . . It carries you from coast to coast . . . And to the farthest
shore . . . It gathers all the world's events . . . And brings them
to your door . . . With more details and background and . . .
More colorful narration . . . Than any other means on earth
. . . For quick communication . . . And it has editorials . . .
And many comic strips . . . The sports reviews, some kitchen
news . . . And health and beauty tips . . . Then add to these
the many ads . . . Display and classified . . . Your local newspaper is bound . . . To be your joy and pride.

WE THANK AND HONOR

We honor those who died for us . . . To each his special grave . . . As much as he was loyal and . . . As surely he was brave . . . He gave his life in combat for . . . Our freedom of today . . . And in that final picture there . . . Is nothing more to say . . . His cross may be at Valley Forge . . . Or deep in Flanders Field . . . At Normandy or anywhere . . . He may have dropped his shield . . . It does not matter when or where . . . He died so suddenly . . . He gave his life for freedom and . . . He guarded you and me . . . We thank him for his courage and . . . His every tear and smile . . . And promise him to carry on . . . And keep his deeds worth while.

MY DATES WITH GOD

I have a constant calendar . . . Inside a metal case . . . And by its turning, every day . . . Is easy to erase . . . I only wish that I could turn . . . The hands of time as well . . . So every clock would start again . . . The story I would tell . . . But as I turn my calendar . . . I know I just pretend . . . And as tomorrow is today . . . So yesterday must end . . . No calendar can stop the clock . . . Of what there is to be . . . And I give thanks to God for all . . . That he has given me . . . And so my calendar is one . . . I hope my prayers fulfill . . . And may His blessing be on me . . . According to His will.

DON'S SHOES

Today I made a special trip . . . To have Don's shoes repaired
. . . I did not care about the cost . . . Or how the price compared . . . I do not mean that I am rich . . . With cash to throw
away . . . Or that my son could never do . . . Without his shoes
today . . . I mean that he must blaze his trail . . . And stand
in his own shoes . . . According to his courage and . . . His
chance to win or lose . . . His future is his own to make . . .
In keeping with his will . . . And every promise he declares
. . . Is one he must fulfill . . . And all that I can do for him
. . . However he may fare . . . Is just to keep the shoes he has
. . . In reasonable repair.

IF ONLY IN MY MIND

My mind is filled with memories . . . Of all we used to know
. . . The streets, the buildings and the park . . . Where often
we would go . . . The walks we took while holding hands . . .
The loving words we said . . . About the possibility . . . That
someday we would wed . . . We passed a thousand persons,
dear . . . And yet we were alone . . . For they were merely
strangers and . . . The world was all our own . . . You were
the only object that . . . My eyes could ever see . . . And by
your actions you revealed . . . That you belonged to me . . . If
only every memory . . . Could be a dream come true . . . My
happiness would be complete . . . In my sweet thoughts of you.

THE WORLD GOES ON

If you turn on the radio . . . Or read the paper through . . .
And everything around the world . . . Seems horrible to you
. . . Remember now that yesterday. . . The news was quite the
same . . . With here and there a different twist . . . Or someone else's name . . . And yet when yesterday was gone . . .
The world did not collapse . . . Your dreams were still quite
possible . . . Your hopes were still "perhaps" . . . There will
be tragedies to face . . . With every night and dawn . . .
But life on earth and human hearts . . . Will keep right going
on . . . So there is nothing now to fear . . . Beyond your moral
way . . . And how Almighty God decrees . . . For you on
Judgment Day.

MY ROSE FOREVER

Oh, I remember when we walked . . . Along the avenue . . .
And when I held your hand in mine . . . And promised to be
true . . . And I remember, darling, when . . . I took you in
my arms . . . And in that loving kiss I felt . . . I gathered all
your charms . . . You were the only creature in . . . The whole
wide world for me . . . As I would share my life with you
. . . For all eternity . . . Yes, I remember, though the wind
. . . Has blown the blooms away . . . Of all the flowers that
belonged . . . To our own yesterday . . . The years have passed
but in my heart . . . Eternally there grows . . . The flower of
your loveliness . . . My everlasting rose.

HOW OFT TO CHURCH?

How often do you go to church? . . . How often do you pray?
. . . And when you turn your thoughts to God . . . What are
the words you say? . . . Do you express your gratitude . . . For
all that He has done . . . To help you conquer obstacles . . . In
battles you have won? . . . Or do you go to church because . . .
It seems the thing to do . . . And maybe, superstitiously . . .
It spells good luck to you? . . . There is no game of any kind
. . . That you can play with God . . . But as you serve Him
well, you will . . . Receive His gracious nod . . . And as you
worship in His house . . . And honor Him today . . . He will
reward you for your love . . . And for your friendly way.

BEHIND HIS BACK

However we resent someone . . . Whatever he may lack . . .
We should not be so cruel as . . . To talk behind his back . . .
We should not take advantage of . . . His absence anywhere
. . . To tell our low opinion and . . . The hatred we would
bare . . . He may deserve our judgment or . . . Perhaps a better
deal . . . But surely he should not be tried . . . By just the way
we feel . . . We should not stoop to criticize . . . His character
or mind . . . If only for the reason that . . . Our words would
be unkind . . . There is a proper time and place . . . For us to
testify . . . But no excuse to gossip or . . . To scorn and vilify.

MY DADDY

A daddy is a darling, as . . . A daddy ought to be . . . But mine
is someone special who . . . Is extra good to me . . . He has to
earn the daily bread . . . That feeds our humble home . . . And
there is never time for him . . . To ramble or to roam . . .
He gives his time to all of us . . . When he is at our side . . .
And only in our happiness . . . Does he have any pride . . .
He does not want a medal or . . . The very least of fame
. . . But just the knowledge in his heart . . . That "Daddy"
is his name . . . Oh, Daddy, I adore you and . . . With all
my heart I say . . . I am so glad that no one else . . . Could
take your place today.

MY MOTHER

My mother is an angel, she . . . Is sweet as she can be . . .
There is not anything on earth . . . She would not do for me
. . . She gives me all the minutes and . . . The hours of her
day . . . And if I am in trouble, she . . . Is on her knees to pray
. . . She thinks of me from early dawn . . . Until the setting
sun . . . And through the night and in her dreams . . . I am
her cherished one . . . She does not wonder what to do . . .
She does not ask me why . . . She only hopes I have the truth
. . . To look her in the eye . . . Oh, Mother, I am grateful for
. . . Your love and faith in me . . . And may I be your child
and God's . . . For all eternity.

CONTEST

A contest is important at . . . The moment that we start . . .
But after it is over, it . . . Should not affect the heart . . . For
it is just a pleasant way . . . To test ability . . . And there is
nothing final in . . . Defeat or victory . . . It merely marks the
score cards for . . . The ones who vied today . . . And sometime
later there will be . . . Another chance to play . . . No victory
can make a mark . . . That will endure forever . . . And what
defeat does not deserve . . . Another good endeavor? . . . Indeed our daily life is just . . . A contest, side by side . . . And
every moment we should try . . . To take it in our stride.

OFFICE POLITICS

In every kind of business you . . . Will find those certain
cliques . . . Or individuals who deal . . . In office politics . . .
Who seek to influence the boss . . . Against the other guy . . .
By every underhanded means . . . And always on the sly . . .
They think that all they have to do . . . Is make someone the
goat . . . Of any blunder that occurs . . . And thereby cut his
throat . . . And if that underdog should get . . . A bright
idea or two . . . They try to steal the credit for . . . A job they
did not do . . . A few of them get by with it . . . And break
somebody's heart . . . But most of them discover that . . .
The boss is much too smart.

WHO WRITE THE ADS

When I read advertising that . . . Appears throughout the
land . . . I know that it was written by . . . A male or female
hand . . . The copy that a man composed . . . Is frank and
aimed to win . . . With usually the cold approach . . . That
marks it masculine . . . Whereas the copywriter who . . . Is on
the distaff side . . . Will take you in her confidence . . . With
nothing left to hide . . . And with the soft, inviting words . . .
That only she can choose . . . You know that sales resistance is
. . . The battle you will lose . . . She has a way of telling you
. . . There could not be a crisis . . . Because the poorest family
. . . Could pay those bargain prices.

I PROMISE YOU

I promise you that I will do . . . Whatever you may ask . . .
No matter what the sacrifice . . . How tiresome the task . . .
If you will give yourself to me . . . In every loving way . . . Not
just tonight, tomorrow but . . . Forever and a day . . . If you
will be my love for life . . . And never ask me why . . . Sometimes the moonlight disappears . . . And stars desert the sky
. . . If only you will trust in me . . . However dark the night
. . . I promise you each morning will . . . Be filled with sunshine bright . . . I promise you as much as I . . . Am able to
bestow . . . Because you are so gentle and . . . Because I love
you so.

BEFORE YOU JUDGE

Let not your heart be guided by . . . The rumors that you hear
. . . But give the victim every chance . . . To prove he is sincere . . . Let not your mind be poisoned by . . . The darts some
people throw . . . Investigate and try to find . . . The facts you
ought to know . . . It is so easy to condemn . . . And play a
dirty game . . . To manufacture lies and to . . . Besmirch a
worthy name . . . Be careful when you read reports . . . Or
hear them on the air . . . Some words escape the censors and
. . . They could be quite unfair . . . Be careful in your judgment of . . . The rumors you receive . . . And take your time
before you choose . . . The things that you believe.

WE DRIFT APART

The friendships of our early youth . . . Quite often disappear
. . . As we grow up, get married and . . . Go on from year to
year . . . Our interests are divided and . . . We sort of drift
away . . . From all the magic pleasures of . . . Our carefree
yesterday . . . We do not feel as close to them . . . As friendships used to be . . . For we are more concerned with our . . .
Immediate family . . . And if our friends stay single, it . . . Is
even likelier . . . That we will gather other folks . . . As friends
whom we prefer . . . Because a friendship made in youth . . .
However we are fond . . . Unless we grow together, is . . .
A temporary bond.

ALL I COULD ASK

I do not ask for anything . . . I do not weep or sigh . . . I do not
wish on any star . . . That decorates the sky . . . Why should I
covet anything . . . However old or new . . . When I have all
the world because . . . I know that I have you? . . . You are my
everything, my love . . . You are my very all . . . Today, and
then tomorrow and . . . Each song that I recall . . . I have
your loving promise, your . . . Abiding faith in me . . . Your
daily inspiration and . . . Your constant sympathy . . . What
more is there to ask of God . . . As human beings live? . . .
And in return I give myself . . . As much as I can give.

WORTH WAITING

When we must paint our house or we . . . Remodel it a bit
. . . The task seems like eternity . . . Until we finish it . . .
Day after day the brushes swish . . . From varicolored pails
. . . The saw is cutting boards in two . . . Or hammers pound
on nails . . . But when the work is over and . . . At last we
settle down . . . We know that it was worth it to . . . Enhance
our place in town . . . And after while our restlessness . . . Has
vanished in the air . . . As house improvements seem as though
. . . They always had been there . . . The same as tears that
disappear . . . The moment we are glad . . . And in our
memory that joy . . . Is all we ever had.

ACTRESS KRISTINA

Kristina is an actress now . . . With all her heart and soul . . .
As all agree who saw her in . . . Her first dramatic role . . .
She acted very natural . . . And never missed a line . . . And if
rehearsals tired her . . . She showed not any sign . , . But also
now her acting has . . . Created quite a stir . . . For it is obvious
to us . . . The bug has bitten her . . . She wants to be a star
someday . . . And see her name in lights . . . And by all standards of the stage . . . To reach the greatest heights . . . And as
Kristina is prepared . . . To struggle for success . . . We wish
our darling 12-year-old . . . A world of happiness.

GOD BLESS OUR U.S.A.

God bless our 13 colonies . . . And bless our land today . . .
And bless each state, all 48 . . . Of our great U.S.A. . . . God
bless our fight for freedom in . . . The days of long ago . . .
When tyranny attempted to . . . Put out our candle's glow
. . . Today we are a nation strong . . . With truth and liberty
. . . With justice and with equal rights . . . For all humanity
. . . In God we trust, and by His grace . . . Our flag will top
the mast . . . As long as there is brotherhood . . . And right-
eousness may last . . . God bless the country of our birth . . .
Or our adopted land . . . And may our democratic way . . . Be
always in command.

ANOTHER LINK

My letter was not finished, dear . . . When last I wrote to you
. . . About my heartfelt gratitude . . . For all the things you
do . . . And I could never finish it . . . As much as ink and
time . . . With any paragraphs of prose . . . Or little lines of
rhyme . . . There is no form of manuscript . . . Or any words
so real . . . That could describe to you, my love . . . The happiness I feel . . . The happiness of knowing you . . . And
sometimes being near . . . Where every word you whisper is
. . . A thought that I can hear . . . And so as I adore you in
. . . The sunshine and the rain . . . I hope this letter adds a
link . . . To love's eternal chain.

VITAL STATISTICS

Without statistics vital and . . . The person at their head . . .
You could not claim that you were born . . . Or prove that
you are dead . . . You never walked upon this earth . . . You
never went away . . . Although your relatives and friends . . .
Were with you every day . . . There is no entry of your birth
. . . No record of your death . . . And so it is quite certain
that . . . You never drew a breath . . . Your signature, your
presence and . . . Your picture on a page . . . May never prove
your birth or death . . . Or intermediate age . . . And yet
statistics vital are . . . Important as can be . . . To keep some
record on the growth . . . Of each community.

FORMULA

The formula is something that . . . Prescribes a certain course
. . . Like medicine, a way to live . . . Or betting on a horse
. . . It is supposed to guide your mind . . . And help you to
survive . . . And yet sometimes without it you . . . Are so much
more alive . . . The formula is handy when . . . There is no
other way . . . And by some chance of circumstance . . . It
still could save the day . . . But sometimes you are better off
. . . When you are on your own . . . Without a method tried
and true . . . Just by yourself—alone . . . And as you try your
fledgling wings . . . It may turn out that you . . . Have found
a special formula . . . Quite wonderful and new.

FORGETFUL WIFE

"Where are my glasses and my keys? . . . Where did I leave
my purse?" . . . Sometimes I think my wife should have . . .
A guardian or a nurse . . . She wanders up the stairs and down
. . . In search of things mislaid . . . And sometimes actually
believes . . . They just got up and strayed . . . "I'm sure I
left it here or there . . . It has to be some place" . . . And yet it
does not come to light . . . Nor is there any trace . . . And so
it goes from day to day . . . While I must stand the cost . . . Of
duplicating articles . . . That suddenly get lost . . . I wish she
had a special place . . . To keep each little thing . . . And,
after that, I wish that she . . . Would be remembering.

HOW TRUE ARE YOU?

How many friends have you today . . . As friends are really true? . . . How many would respond at once . . . To testify for you? . . . How many would defend you in . . . The face of accusation . . . And would unhesitatingly . . . Accept your explanation? . . . Or if you lost your income and . . . You had to have some aid . . . How many still would measure up . . . To earn that friendship grade? . . . Some day you may discover that . . . Your true friends are not many . . . And you may feel quite fortunate . . . To find that you have any . . . But meanwhile think of those who think . . . You will be ever true . . . And when their trial is at hand . . . They can depend on you.

OFFICE COLLECTION

It seems they ask for money in . . . The office every day . . . For someone getting married or . . . A baby on its way . . . To cheer a fellow-worker who . . . Has had an operation . . . Or just to help an oldster on . . . His permanent vacation . . . It may be for a birthday or . . . To compensate some loss . . . Or buy a little present for . . . A kind, congenial boss . . . It seems to be a malady . . . That has its own infection . . . As office forces carry on . . . To make each new collection . . . You do not have to give to it . . . You need not pay a cent . . . But if you do, may God bless you . . . For your good sentiment.

AS WE MAY ROAM

When we are young and free of heart . . . We sort of like to roam . . . To leave our daily neighborhood . . . And get away from home . . . To mingle with the outer world . . . That seems to be more wise . . . And try sophistication out . . . According to our size . . . Well, some of us can do it and . . . Achieve a real success . . . With wealth and popularity . . . And every happiness . . . But some of us become a flop . . . A failure from the start . . . Because the world of glamor is . . . Not suited to our heart . . . Those some of us are those of us . . . Who never ought to roam . . . Who are much better off to live . . . A humble life at home.

IT MEANS SO MUCH

Your love means more to me than just . . . The joy of knowing you . . . And more than all the happiness . . . Of wanting to to be true . . . It means that now I have a chance . . . To show you that I care . . . And that my heart and all I have . . . Are always yours to share . . . That nothing is important in . . . My life from day to day . . . Unless you like it, and it makes . . . You happy in some way . . . I want to live for you, my love . . . And live for you alone . . . As long as you embrace me and . . . I am your very own . . . Your love means more to me than all . . . The treasures there may be . . . Because it is the dearest prize . . . That could belong to me.

AS STRONG AS GRACE

My courage is my faith in God . . . As now I hope to win . . .
My only fear is weakness, as . . . I try to conquer sin . . .
I know that I am soft and frail . . . As human beings are . . .
And yet my hands reach out to touch . . . That everlasting star
. . . The star that guides me to the goal . . . That God has set
for me . . . Where I may share His kingdom great . . . For
all eternity . . . My hands reach out in fervent prayer . . .
For that enduring grace . . . And all the strength I need to
meet . . . The problems I must face . . . Because in courage,
faith and hope . . . Wherever I may plod . . . I am no stronger
than the grace . . . That I receive from God.

OLD NEIGHBORHOOD

I like to travel many miles . . . And visit places new . . . To
study local customs and . . . Observe what people do . . . It is
refreshing to my mind . . . And I learn many things . . . Of
fascinating history . . . And current happenings . . . But there
are times when I prefer . . . The neighborhoods I know . . .
That hold a thousand memories . . . Of days so long ago . . .
I like to walk along each street . . . Of some familiar name
. . . That is so different now, and yet . . . Is somehow still the
same . . . The neighborhoods that in my heart . . . Have
lingered through the years . . . With hopes and dreams and
happy songs . . . And all their smiles and tears.

HOW WISE THE OWL?

The owl may look intelligent . . . With eyes that stare and blink . . . But it is not as wise a bird . . . As many people think . . . It cannot match the raven or . . . The goose or any crow . . . In using common faculties . . . As feathered creatures go . . . It cannot see in daylight, or . . . At least not very good . . . And it must move its head around . . . To see the neighborhood . . . The owl may howl and it may screech . . . And it may haunt the park . . . And scare a person half to death . . . While walking in the dark . . . But it is not intelligent . . . Despite its solemn eyes . . . The same as many humans who . . . May seem but are not wise.

PERSONAL FREEDOM

There is no moral justice in . . . The law that would deny . . . The freedom that is personal . . . As life is passing by . . . The inhibitions and the acts . . . In seriousness or fun . . . That are not carried out to harm . . . Or bother anyone . . . In other words, the private life . . . That is pursued alone . . . Which certainly in every way . . . Should be the person's own . . . For if that privilege is abused . . . There are those laws today . . . That rule the action wrongful and . . . The guilty has to pay . . . And so in legislative trends . . . It should be kept in sight . . . That individual freedom is . . . A basic human right.

NO AFFIDAVIT

I need no affidavit or . . . A signature from you . . . To make
it positive for me . . . That you are really true . . . I see it in
your soulful eyes . . . I hear it in your voice . . . And by your
deep devotion, dear . . . I know I am your choice . . . Your
whispers and your gestures as . . . We walk along the street
. . . Your arms around my shoulders and . . . Your lips so
soft and sweet . . . In all the ways that love can speak . . .
Your heart has made it clear . . . That you belong to me, my
love . . . Forever and a year . . . I need no affidavit, dear
. . . Or other public oath . . . To seal the loving promises
. . . That bind and bless us both.

HANG UP!

What is more irritating than . . . To wait upon a phone . . .
While it is being kept in use . . . By someone young or grown?
. . . The person in a public booth . . . Who hesitates and
stalls . . . Or keeps on putting coins in slots . . . To make a
dozen calls . . . Or in the comfort of your home . . . The
daughter or the son . . . Who has a most important date . . .
Or homework to be done . . . You get exasperated and . . .
You want to yell or whine . . . And there is mayhem in your
heart . . . As you would grab that line . . . You do not want
to cut them short . . . With only half a cup . . . But in all
fairness to your ears . . . You wish they would hang up.

I ENVY PRETZEL

I wish that I were Pretzel, with . . . His soft and easy way
. . . To eat and drink and run around . . . And sleep both
night and day . . . I wish I were a dachshund small . . .
As Pretzel is our pet . . . With never any care in life . . . Or
trouble to forget . . . To have somebody care for me . . .
And cuddle me real tight . . . To pat my head and smooth my
hair . . . And tell me nighty-night . . . I wish that I were
Pretzel now . . . Including leash and tag . . . A happy little
puppy with . . . A tail that likes to wag . . . I envy Pretzel,
yet my heart . . . Is happy as can be . . . If I were he, I could
not kiss . . . And hold him close to me.

IMPORTANT TASKS

I make a special memo on . . . Important things to do . . .
And though I struggle every day . . . I never quite get through
. . . I check them off my list as fast . . . As every job is done
. . . But always underneath the next . . . There is another
one . . . And always I am adding things . . . Until I have to
write . . . Another memo of the tasks . . . I ought to expedite
. . . And so it goes from day to day . . . Forever without end
. . . No matter how much energy . . . I constantly expend . . .
But then sometimes I wonder as . . . I tackle something new
. . . How would I feel if I had no . . . Important thing to do?

IF ONLY FOR A WHILE

Again a friend reminded me . . . How many days are few
. . . For him who suddenly becomes . . . A special friend to
you . . . You get together, and you wish . . . Through all
your smiles and tears . . . That you had known each other for
. . . At least a hundred years . . . And then you greet each
other for . . . A little while or so . . . And suddenly there
comes the time . . . For one of you to go . . . Some friendships
last for many years . . . And some for just a day . . . But who
are we to question God . . . And His mysterious way? . . .
And in the last analysis . . . We thank Him with a smile . . .
For one more friendship on this earth . . . If only for a while.

TIME FOR GOD

What does this Sunday mean to you? . . . How much are
you aware . . . It is the day to honor God . . . In every thought
and prayer? . . . What is an hour more or less . . . Of slumber
or of play . . . When life may dangle by the thread . . . Of
just a night or day? . . . Would you prefer your score in golf
. . . Or baseball victory . . . Or any pleasure as against . . .
His great eternity? . . . Then why not take these moments off
. . . Forget your play or sleep . . . And prove to God your
promises . . . Are those you mean to keep? . . . Take just
this little time for God . . . As He takes time for you . . . And
thank Him for His grace in all . . . That He has helped you do.

OUR MINIMUM

Our minimum and maximum . . . Are measurements we
take . . . As we indulge ourselves or live . . . For someone
else's sake . . . So many times we give ourselves . . . The maximum of fun . . . While goodness is the minimum . . . Of
all that we get done . . . We only think about ourselves . . .
We have no use for others . . . As we forget that we were born
. . . As sisters and as brothers . . . Our minimum should be
a prayer . . . That we shall never rest . . . Until we reach the
maximum . . . And do our very best . . . To honor God in
Heaven and . . . Attain eternity . . . As much as we are able
with . . . Our human energy.

HOW MANY DREAMS?

I never go to sleep, my love . . . Without I dream of you . . .
And every day I pray my dreams . . . Will soon be coming true
. . . I wonder in my lonely heart . . . How much you think
of me . . . And if you realize all that you . . . Inspire me to be
. . . I want to be so kind and good . . . So honest, true and
fair . . . I long to gain perfection's goal . . . With every virtue
rare . . . But, oh, how much my hopes depend . . . On what
your lips may say . . . And whether you and I will share . . .
Each other's life someday . . . How many nights and dreams
must I . . . Endure until that dawn? . . . How many days and
weeks will my . . . Uncertainty go on?

WE LOVE YOU SO

I do not count the years that pass . . . I do not keep a score
. . . But every birthday that you have . . . I love you more and
more . . . I love you for your gentleness . . . Your sweetness
and your smile . . . And for the happiness of life . . . That
grows with every mile . . . I love you for our children who . . .
. . . Are pictures of your face . . . But who could never be
more sweet . . . Or ever take your place . . . A happy birthday, darling, from . . . The children and from me . . . And
may this be the brightest day . . . For all our family . . . And
may your years of life on earth . . . Be many, many more . . .
With every moment sweeter than . . . The one you had before.

I AM YOUR GOD

I shall be with you every day . . . Wherever you may be . . .
If you are dressed in common clothes . . . Or in your finery
. . . If you are happy in your heart . . . Or filled with constant
fear . . . That something tragic will occur . . . To those so
near and dear . . . I shall be ever at your side . . . To love
and comfort you . . . However you are right or wrong . . .
In what you try to do . . . I am The Shepherd of your life
. . . If only you regret . . . And as you are forgiving, you . . .
Are willing to forget . . . Remember this each moment of
. . . Your life upon this sod . . . I made you, and I love you,
and . . . I am your only God.

YOUR SACRIFICE

If you would make a sacrifice . . . And do your loving share
. . . Then serve the ones who suffer, with . . . A vigil and a
prayer . . . Keep vigil at their sickbed side . . . Console and
comfort them . . . Your very presence will become . . . A
charitable gem . . . God will reward each minute and . . .
Each second that you spend . . . With any ailing relative . . .
A stranger or a friend . . . And as your lips sincerely shape
. . . The whisper of a prayer . . . You may be sure the patient
is . . . In God's beloved care . . . For as He made the world
to be . . . For sister and for brother . . . So He rewards the
sacrifice . . . We make for one another.

FOREVER, DEAR

My love is yours forever, dear . . . Forever and a day . . .
With all the loving sentiments . . . That I could ever say
. . . My love is yours because I know . . . Your heart belongs
to me . . . And we have promised to be one . . . For all eternity
. . . And in the sweetness of your kiss . . . Whatever storm
or rain . . . I know that my decision, dear . . . Could never
be in vain . . . Because you are so dear and kind . . . I could
not ask for more . . . You are my mountain and my sky . . .
And every moonlit shore . . . And so I offer you my love . . .
And with my heart I say . . . That I am yours forever, dear
. . . Forever and a day.

YOU ARE A NEIGHBOR

When you think about your neighbors . . . Don't forget that
you are theirs . . . That you ought to share a little . . . Of
their burdens and their cares . . . Don't forget that they are
people . . . And they merit your concern . . . So whenever
they befriend you . . . Do some kindness in return . . . They
have problems just as you have . . . And perhaps far greater
too . . . And they may be sacrificing . . . When they do some
deed for you . . . Don't ignore your friendly neighbors . . .
When you do not need their aid . . . You may have an obligation . . . That can never quite be paid . . . Even if you're not
indebted . . . In the normal way we know . . . There is still
your daily duty . . . Just to smile and say hello.

STORY-DREAMS

I read the stories that appear . . . In different magazines . . .
And weigh the possibilities . . . Of those enchanting scenes
. . . The hero and the heroine . . . Are faced with doubt
and fright . . . And always as the plot unfolds . . . They seem
to fare all right . . . I wish that life could be that way . . . As
writers all pretend . . . And every problem on this earth . . .
Would have a happy end . . . But fiction is a dreamland for
. . . The slumber of our youth . . . And it can even cloud
their souls . . . In finding out the truth . . . A story may be
wonderful . . . But nothing takes the place . . . Of cold
realities and all . . . The problems we must face.

UP THE STAIRS

Each time I mount our winding stairs . . . To sleep or change my dress . . . I cannot help but think about . . . The ladder to success . . . I think about the children and . . . Our worries and our cares . . . As bravely in their babyhood . . . They tried to climb those stairs . . . It seemed so high and dangerous . . . But they were not afraid . . . And as they crawled and clambered up . . . They always made the grade . . . Those stairs are like that ladder, for . . . The passing years have shown . . . The real and steady progress of . . . Our children, nearly grown . . . And so the stairway in our home . . . Where baby booties went . . . Is every inch the ladder of . . . Success and sentiment.

LET FREEDOM LIVE

The wars have come, the wars have gone . . . And still we are together . . . America, the beautiful . . . In every kind of weather . . . America, by land and sea . . . From famous Paul Revere . . . To all the battles we have fought . . . To keep tradition dear . . . Today these many years ago . . . We won our liberation . . . And now with eight and forty states . . . We are a mighty nation . . . May God be always with us in . . . Our struggle to be free . . . And show our neighbors what it means . . . To have democracy . . . May every country follow in . . . Our footsteps of example . . . And may there be no enemy . . . Who tries to kill or trample.

EMPLOYES ONLY

Employes serve the public and . . . They have to keep their place . . . But being humble on this earth . . . Is never a disgrace . . . And many times I ask myself . . . Who really wears the crown . . . As men and women stop to shop . . . In stores around the town? . . . While customers are special guests . . . However old or new . . . Employes in another sense . . . Are quite exclusive too . . . There are those signs on doors that make . . . Your soul a little lonely . . . As they inform you that this way . . . Is for "Employes Only" . . . You cannot penetrate that place . . . You cannot go in there . . . Not even if your buying name . . . Is Mr. Millionaire.

HER MUSIC STAND

Sometime ago Kristina put . . . Her clarinet away . . . And with it went the stand that held . . . The songs she used to play . . . And I was sorry, not because . . . Of money I had spent . . . But just because she did so well . . . Upon that instrument . . . It seemed to be a tragedy . . . That I had come across . . . Yet, now, at least her music stand . . . Is not a total loss . . . I use it to rehearse a speech . . . That I must give today . . . Or else to memorize my lines . . . For some forthcoming play . . . And as I fondly handle it . . . I have no real regret . . . Somehow I feel Kristina will . . . Resume her clarinet.

PRAYER FOR WISDOM

I ask You, God, for wisdom good . . . To guide my heart and soul . . . That I may fill my place on earth . . . And I may reach my goal . . . I do not want the wisdom, God . . . That leads to prominence . . . But just the kind that faithful souls . . . Consider common sense . . . The common sense to understand . . . That life belongs to You . . . And only by Your loving grace . . . Is anything we do . . . The wisdom to be faithful and . . . To serve Your holy will . . . To choose the right from wrong, and all . . . My promises fulfill . . . I pray to You for wisdom, God . . . To do the best I can . . . To prove I love You by the way . . . I love my fellowman.

COST OF ILLNESS

The cost of illness can be high . . . In any family . . . Especially in hospitals . . . With need for surgery . . . It can destroy the budget and . . . Exhaust the last reserve . . . And it can be distressing to . . . The smallest human nerve . . . But if it helps to save a life . . . Or make its suffering less . . . Its payment is a sacrifice . . . That will bring happiness . . . It is a deed of love that is . . . Most pleasing to The Lord . . . And somehow and eventually . . . Receives a rich reward . . . It is the bread of kindness that . . . Is cast upon the sea . . . And finds its way to shore again . . . On waves of charity.

DAWN IN SUMMER

In summertime I like to rise . . . Before the dawn is here . . .
And watch the darkness leave the sky . . . And slowly disappear . . . All nature seems to stir itself . . . Without the slightest sound . . . Except the singing of the birds . . . Above the
waking ground . . . And then bright colors start to blend . . .
Across the morning sky . . . Before the sun is visible . . . To
any human eye . . . That is the hour when I like . . . To meditate and dream . . . And contemplate the nobler side . . . Of
life's unending stream . . . To count my blessings on this
earth . . . And thank my God again . . . That such as I may
share His world . . . With all my fellowmen.

BURY THE BLAME

How many times have I been wrong? . . . How many times
have you? . . . How often dear, should we divide . . . The
blame between us two? . . . Sometimes I think the fault is
yours . . . And I condemn you for it . . . But when the guilt
is clearly mine . . . You never seem to score it . . . And therein
lies the answer to . . . Our stubbornness and strife . . . The
way to solve our problems and . . . Pursue a peaceful life
. . . It matters not so much that you . . . And I have failed
each other . . . As being willing to forgive . . . And cherish
one another . . . "To err is human," to forgive . . . Is said to
be divine . . . So may I lose your least mistake . . . As you
have buried mine.

WHAT WORTH REGRET?

What is the value of regret? . . . Is it a virtue true? . . . If
you are sorry for a wrong . . . What does it mean to you? . . .
If you regret and go your way . . . And think of it no more . . .
Then surely no reward will be . . . Presented at your door
. . . You will be nothing better than . . . Your heart has ever
been . . . And you will not be worthy of . . . Forgiveness for
your sin . . . Regret is not a virtue true . . . Unless your soul
atones . . . For hurling thoughts and words of hate . . . Or
casting cruel stones . . . Unless you are sincerely sad . . .
It ever happened then . . . And firmly promise God that it
. . . Will not occur again.

SONGS AT HOME

It seems an ancient custom by . . . The habits of today . . .
But once upon a time we loved . . . To hear pianos play . . .
Not those that graced the concert halls . . . Of marble walls
and domes . . . But those down-payment instruments . . .
That stood in common homes . . . Where dad and mom and
all the kids . . . Would sort of bunch around . . . And they
would join in singing songs . . . However they might sound
. . . There was no operatic voice . . . Or genius on the way
. . . But there was something special that . . . You could not
buy today . . . The happiness of home and hearth . . . Regardless of the weather . . . Where just a little song could keep
. . . The family together.

PIECE OF PAPER

A piece of paper may be just . . . An unimportant scrap . . .
Or it may be the evidence . . . That sets a deadly trap . . . It
may be just the portion of . . . A letter never mailed . . . Or
it may tell the tragedy . . . Of somebody who failed . . . The
corner of a love-note or . . . A murderer's confession . . . A
piece of paper can be quite . . . A damaging expression . . .
Or it may tell the number of . . . A certain telephone . . .
Our teen-age youths are ringing when . . . They want to
talk alone . . . A piece of paper may be just . . . A thing to
toss away . . . Or it may play the vital part . . . To lose or
save the day.

AS YOU ARE FRIENDS

In friendship there is happiness . . . But it depends on two
. . . And you must serve your friend as well . . . As you would
have him do . . . There must be handshake in success . . .
And comfort in defeat . . . And taking equal turns to set . . .
The time and place to meet . . . In friendship there is never
room . . . For any jealousy . . . For doubt, distrust or any
form . . . Of insincerity . . . There is no ear for gossip and
. . . No tongue to criticize . . . Nor ever any reason to . . .
Assume the least disguise . . . And only as you disappoint . . .
And really fail your friend . . . Or as he proves untrue to you
. . . Will friendship ever end.

GLAD YOU WERE BORN

What makes a birthday special? . . . Why do you send a card?
. . . It is not just remembrance or . . . Your personal regard
. . . It is the fact that you are glad . . . That he or she is
here . . . Because that someone has become . . . A person
very dear . . . You do not celebrate the dawn . . . Of one
more birthday morn . . . But you are grateful unto God . . .
That such a soul was born . . . So keep this little thought in
mind . . . The next time that you send . . . A happy birthday
greeting to . . . A relative or friend . . . That you are joyful
in your heart . . . For someone very dear . . . And joyful for
yourself because . . . That one is really here.

FOR YOU AND GOD

My thoughts of you are not the thoughts . . . Of passion and
desire . . . The greed and the cupidity . . . That set the mind
on fire . . . They are the elevated thoughts . . . Of incense
in the air . . . That seek to join our hearts with God . . . In
everlasting prayer . . . To carry out the will of God . . . As
we fulfill the duty . . . Of matrimony on this earth . . . In
all its love and beauty . . . To walk together every mile . . .
To sleep and eat and drink . . . To smile and suffer side by
side . . . And share the thoughts we think . . . My thoughts,
my dreams, my hopes, my faith . . . My very least endeavor
. . . Are all for you and God, that we . . . May honor Him
forever.

WHAT IS TIME?

What is the element of time . . . As we pursue our way? . . .
Is it the ticking of the clock . . . As night must follow day?
. . . Is time no more than passing life . . . And just to wait
and see . . . Each momentary happening . . . Become a memory? . . . No, time is that important thing . . . That regulates
the scope . . . Of every effort, firm resolve . . . And every
dream and hope . . . It is the period of life . . . We are allowed
on earth . . . To walk away from virtue or . . . To prove
our lasting worth . . . The element of time is that . . . Which
finally must end . . . Where God alone decides who is . . .
His enemy or friend.

FOR ALL THE YOUNG

For all the children on this earth . . . I say this prayer today
. . . That they may learn The Lord, our God . . . And live
His holy way . . . The children of the city and . . . The quiet
countryside . . . And unto every jungle where . . . The igno-
rant abide . . . Each baby that is given birth . . . Belongs to
God at last . . . Today, tomorrow and throughout . . . Each
moment of the past . . . I pray for all the childen who . . .
Are playing everywhere . . . That they will be forever in
. . . His kind and loving care . . . That every child will learn
the truth . . . Wherever it may plod . . . And in its every
sacrifice . . . To give itself to God.

PICTURE-PAST

A photo or a snapshot is . . . A picture of the past . . . To
help preserve some memory . . . As long as it may last . . .
It is a certain likeness we . . . May never see again . . . As
youthful and as wonderful . . . As everything was then . . .
Or it may be a recent view . . . Of old or middle age . . . For
children or grandchildren as . . . They turn another page
. . . Each one has some important place . . . However small
it seems . . . Inside the family album of . . . Our memories
and dreams . . . It is a preservation of . . . The days we used
to know . . . Familiar faces yesterday . . . And those of long
ago.

HOLD YOUR PEN

How carefully do you prepare . . . A letter that you send . . .
When you are writing to a firm . . . A relative or friend?
. . . Are you as kind and courteous . . . As you should always
be? . . . Or are you careless with your pen . . . And write
it hastily? . . . If you are not concerned about . . . The way
you write a letter . . . You ought to stop and think sometime
. . . And try to write it better . . . Remember that your signature . . . Is like a fingerprint . . . It will identify your
thoughts . . . In every word and hint . . . So do be careful
when you write . . . At least be diplomatic . . . Your phrases
and your sentences . . . Could cause a lot of static.

EMBRACE ME, LOVE

How many phrases fill my pen . . . With words that I can
say . . . To let you know how much, my love . . . You mean
in every way? . . . How many dreams are there in life? . . .
How many stars above? . . . How many numerals exist . . .
To multiply my love? . . . My thoughts of you are countless,
and . . . My hopes and wishes, too . . . As are my constant
praises and . . . The prayers I say for you . . . What more
do you desire, dear? . . . What promise would you ask . . .
As much as I am willing to . . . Fulfill whatever task? . . . I
am your own for evermore . . . As much as I can be . . . As
long as you embrace me, love . . . And you are true to me.

WE SING YOUR GLORY

Our hearts rejoice with You, O Lord . . . Who rose this Easter
Day . . . Hosanna to The Son of God . . . As now we kneel
and pray . . . We praise You and we worship You . . . Eternal
Lord and God . . . And ask You to forgive us for . . . Our
sins upon this sod . . . We thank You for Your sufferings . . .
And promise You today . . . That we will truly try to live . . .
According to Your way . . . O Jesus Christ, Who died for us
. . . Please listen to our prayer . . . And help us to be worthy
of . . . Your kind and loving care . . . We join Your resur-
rection with . . . The angels at Your grave . . . And sing
Your glory for the souls . . . You came on earth to save.

SHE WAS SO KIND

A friend of mine passed on today . . . I did not know her long
. . . But, oh, her heart was happy and . . . Her voice was like
a song . . . She was so kind to everyone . . . So lovable and
sweet . . . To relatives, acquaintances . . . And strangers on
the street . . . She seemed to live her life for God . . . By
being good to others . . . As she considered all the world . . .
Her sisters and her brothers . . . My heart is filled with tears
today . . . Remembering her smile . . . And how she sought
no glory but . . . She loved the rank and file . . . And all I
hope and pray is this . . . That all who knew her name . . .
Will take up her example and . . . Will try to be the same.

MY PRIVATE STUDY

My wife insists my study is . . . A special place for me . . .
Where I may labor undisturbed . . . By any company . . . She
has it air-conditioned when . . . The summer days are hot
. . . And heated in the winter when . . . The cold is quite
a lot . . . And as I sit behind my desk . . . And struggle more
and more . . . I do enjoy the temperature . . . Inside my
study door . . . But so does all the family . . . And everyone
who calls . . . As they are made to feel at home . . . Within
my study walls . . . And so with every snowflake or . . . The
scorching of the sun . . . You can imagine how much work
. . . I'm lucky to get done.

FOREVER ALONE

No matter what you ask of me . . . I never will say "no" . . . Wherever you would guide me, dear . . . I certainly will go . . . I am your own forever as . . . I give my love to you . . . And promise you with all my heart . . . As much as I can do . . . The only thing I ask of you . . . By way of some return . . . Is that there is no other one . . . For whom you ever yearn . . . Give me the promise that there are . . . No shadows in the skies . . . Or anyone more favorable . . . To gaze into your eyes . . . I want you for myself, my dear . . . I want you for my own . . . Forever as my helpmate and . . . Forever all alone.

FAMILY CIRCLE

The family circle of itself . . . Is not a solid ring . . . It is a chain comprised of links . . . Where each means everything . . . It is a circle only as . . . Each link is strong and fast . . . And only as their mettle and . . . Their unity will last . . . It need not be a ring of steel . . . It can be made of flowers . . . As much as there is love to give . . . In sacrificing hours . . . But there must be no sister sad . . . Or brother who offends . . . And parents must not interfere . . . With sudden choice of friends . . . The family circle is a chain . . . With every link a part . . . Of happiness and love that shapes . . . A ring around the heart.

WINDOW

The window is a sheet of glass . . . That lets in daily light . . .
And lets the ones at home behold . . . The silver stars at
night . . . It is a guardian against . . . The wind and snow and
rain . . . Although against a hailstorm it . . . May be a fragile
pane . . . To some it offers pictures of . . . The neighbors
passing by . . . Providing satisfaction for . . . The gossip's
nosey eye . . . Or it may mark a show-place where . . . The
drapes are never drawn . . . So all the poor may ogle and . . .
The rich may see their lawn . . . In any case, the window
serves . . . Both commoner and queen . . . And it is not much
use to us . . . Unless we keep it clean.

FELLOW TRAVELER

I like the "fellow traveler" . . . I try to be one, too . . . But not
the kind of character . . . That may occur to you . . . I do
not mean the foreign spy . . . Who sports a "party card" . . .
Or traitors in our ranks who try . . . To get us off our guard
. . . I mean the fellow traveler . . . Who does not hesitate
. . . To be a friendly traveler . . . Before it is too late . . .
Who joins in conversation on . . . A train or bus or plane . . .
And makes me feel my travel-time . . . Is quite a social gain
. . . Who does not sit there, glum and cold . . . Without a
word to say . . . And on arrival, grabs his hat . . . And hurries
on his way.

NO RIGHT TO DIE

I have no right to take my life . . . For it belongs to God . . .
As much as He created me . . . And placed me on this sod
. . . He gave me all the freedom of . . . The will I have today
. . . To strive for some important goal . . . Or fool my time
away . . . To make my careful choice between . . . The goals
of love and hate . . . And try to find my place among . . . The
humble and the great . . . God has His own design for me
. . . Yet it is mine to choose . . . As I may gamble recklessly
. . . And I may win or lose . . . But even in my darkest
mood . . . And my most trying strife . . . I must remember
that I have . . . No right to take my life.

MY DREAM COME TRUE

This is the fullness of my life . . . My sweetest dream come
true . . . As I have asked in every prayer . . . The joy of
loving you . . . The joy of being at your side . . . Whatever
night or day . . . Of kissing you and listening to . . . The
precious words you say . . . The happiness of every smile
. . . That you bestow on me . . . And every picture painted
in . . . My book of memory . . . What more could I desire,
dear? . . . What riches to be had? . . . I have the treasure of
your heart . . . To be forever glad . . . While now I strive
with all my soul . . . To make you happy, too . . . As you have
given me your love . . . So I belong to you.

Dear daughter, Kris, this day we wish . . . The best in life
for you . . . With every real and true success . . . In all you
strive to do . . . God bless you, sweet Kristina, for . . . The
lovely girl you are . . . With charm and poise and talent that
. . . Deserve a special star . . . Your fourteenth birthday
means so much . . . To Mommy and to me . . . As now it
brings that added joy . . . To our fond memory . . . Our
memory of every day . . . So filled with warmth and cheer
. . . Because of you—so lovable . . . So good and so sincere
. . . God bless you on your birthday for . . . Our fourteen
years of bliss . . . And long and happy be your life . . . Our
darling daughter, Kris.

BE GENTLE

Whatever are your prospects as . . . The world may offer you
. . . Be sure you are a gentle soul . . . In everything you
do . . . Be kind and courteous to those . . . Who may be cold
and curt . . . Politeness is a quality . . . That cannot ever hurt
. . . There is no gain from getting mad . . . Nor happiness
in spite . . . And it is so much easier . . . For you to be polite
. . . You may not be the leader that . . . Your neighbors
would select . . . But you will be in high regard . . . And
have your self-respect . . . So try to be a gentle soul . . . In
every way you can . . . As God Himself would have you love
. . . And serve your fellowman.

TYPEWRITER

Typewriters are so wonderful . . . I use one every day . . .
And take my portable along . . . Each time I go away . . .
Indeed throughout my travels far . . . It keeps me company
. . . And if I left it home, my wife . . . Would seldom hear
from me . . . Because it is so tiring . . . To write a lengthy
letter . . . With pen or pencil, when those keys . . . Are faster
and much better . . . And my dear wife is just the same . . .
She must have her machine . . . To keep me posted constantly
. . . On our domestic scene . . . Typewritten words are legible
. . . And easy on the eyes . . . And by their natural neatness
they . . . Encourage prompt replies.

ON YOUR VACATION

Wherever you vacation, dear . . . I wish you all the best . . .
I hope you will enjoy yourself . . . And get a lot of rest . . .
I wish that I could be with you . . . Along the oceanside
. . . High on a mountain, by a lake . . . Or anywhere
you hide . . . But my vacation time this year . . . Is not the
same as yours . . . And so it seems we are compelled . . . To
take our separate tours . . . I wish you well, and yet I hope
. . . By every moon and sun . . . You find no better image
of . . . Your one and only one . . . For I'll be lonely and I
will . . . Be waiting at your door . . . To tell your heart a
thousand times . . . I love you more and more.

GOD STOPS THE CLOCK

Sometimes when I am weary and . . . I have a task to do . . .
I say a little prayer to God . . . That I may see it through . . .
And then I go on working and . . . The time is growing late
. . . And there are deadlines to be met . . . Those things that
cannot wait . . . But even as I run around . . . In never-ending
hurry . . . I suddenly become aware . . . I did not have to
worry . . . Somehow the job is done on time . . . The promise
is fullfilled . . . And as the seconds disappear . . . My racing
heart is stilled . . . I should have known my little prayer . . .
Was one more share of stock . . . And as I turned my thoughts
to God . . . He surely stopped the clock.

BE A BROTHER

Try to be a real good brother . . . To each person on the street
. . . Speak with kindness to the other . . . Every time you
chance to meet . . . Put your promise into action . . . To
assist some other one . . . And derive the satisfaction . . . Of
a noble deed well done . . . Though it be the smallest favor
. . . That involves no sacrifice . . . It will have the finest
flavor . . . Far beyond the highest price . . . Just a drop of
your devotion . . . To the least upon this sod . . . Will become a boundless ocean . . . On the record kept by God . . .
Be of service, be a brother . . . In the struggle and the strife
. . . Do your best to help another . . . And receive eternal
life.

FORGIVE ME, LORD

Today You sacrificed Your life . . . For all humanity . . .
And in Your mercy, Lord, You died . . . Especially for me
. . . Because I am the least, O Lord . . . Of all your souls
on earth . . . As much as I have shown myself . . . To be of
smallest worth . . . I nailed You to that tree, my Lord . . . I
raised the cross on high . . . More than the soldiers or the
one . . . Who sentenced You to die . . . More than the scribes
and Pharisees . . . Who feared and hated You . . . Because
You taught the word of God . . . The only teaching true . . .
Forgive me, Lord, for all my sins . . . Forgive the fool in me
. . . And give me just a tiny spot . . . In Your eternity.

WE MUST GROW OLD

I wish I were a child again . . . With time to roam and play
. . . I wish that I could walk again . . . The paths of yesterday . . . Without a worry in my heart . . . Or problem on
my mind . . . And only more of happiness . . . And friendliness to find . . . When spring was green, the summer gold
. . . And fall an artist's scheme . . . And winter was a fairy-
land . . . Where we would laugh and dream . . . I wish that
I could put away . . . The burdens that are mine . . . And
be once more that little child . . . Of seven, eight or nine . . .
But time and tide can't be denied . . . As calendars unfold
. . . Our worries weigh, our hair must gray . . . And all of
us grow old.

LAZY KRISSIE

Kristina is a lazy girl . . . She never makes her bed . . . And what she ought to put away . . . Is on the floor instead . . . Her dresses and her dollies and . . . Her games and story books . . . And all the other articles . . . For which our daughter looks . . . And if she wants some food or drink . . . Her only energy . . . Is just to reach the bannister . . . And holler down to me . . . But when she goes to summer camp . . . She waits upon herself . . . And neatly every item small . . . Is stacked upon her shelf . . . I guess we sort of pamper her . . . And yet we have no fear . . . That our affection and our help . . . Will spoil our Krissie dear.

YOUNG MOTHERS

Sometimes young mothers feel that they . . . Are paying quite a price . . . And they would like to emphasize . . . Their wondrous sacrifice . . . They tell about the muddy shoes . . . That mess up every floor . . . The washing and the cooking and . . . The chores for evermore . . . The dinner invitations and . . . The parties all turned down . . . Because no baby sitter is . . . Available in town . . . Well, they are just beginning to . . . Discover sacrifice . . . And year by year their hearts will learn . . . There is no ceiling price . . . But if they keep their courage up . . . And if they persevere . . . They will be wealthy in the words . . . "I love you, Mother dear."

I KNOW YOU LOVE ME

What difference does it make, my love . . . If you propose to me . . . Or if I offer you my heart . . . As long as we may be? . . . I know you love me, and I know . . . My life belongs to you . . . And firmly I believe that we . . . Shall be forever true . . . Why should I wait to hear the words . . . Beneath your bashful smile . . . When I have listened to your heart . . . And known them all the while? . . . Oh, let me hold you in my arms . . . And draw your lips to mine . . . And let this moment be the one . . . When both of us resign . . . Let me embrace you evermore . . . And cuddle to your cheek . . . And in the closeness of our kiss . . . You will not have to speak.

FROM THE HEART

No prayer can come from any lips . . . However much they part . . . Or from the tongue, unless that prayer . . . Is also from the heart . . . A prayer is not a group of words . . . A poem or a song . . . Its measure is not beauty or . . . The lines, however long . . . It is no prose of sacred words . . . Throughout the centuries . . . That promises the grace of God . . . And all His sympathies . . . A prayer is not a prayer unless . . . We mean each word we say . . . And we are humble in our hearts . . . As fervently we pray . . . And whether it is memorized . . . Or suddenly expressed . . . Our prayer sincere will reach God's ear . . . To heed our least request.

LONG LOST FRIEND

A long lost friend may be someone . . . Who vanished long
ago . . . And tried to hide his whereabouts . . . From those
who sought to know . . . But also he may be the one . . .
Who merely went his way . . . And every calendar became
. . . Another yesterday . . . He went his way, and you went
yours . . . The world revolved and then . . . One sudden day
you met and smiled . . . And you shook hands again . . .
A long lost friend may be the one . . . Who searched for you
for years . . . Who loved you and who wanted so . . . To share
your smiles and tears . . . Who looked for you in springtime
and . . . In every autumn frost . . . And dreamed and hoped
to meet again . . . The friend he thought he lost.

PLAYWRIGHT

He sets the stage and weaves the plot . . . For some dramatic
play . . . And he—and only he—can tell . . . The actors what
to say . . . Except as sometimes they ad lib . . . When they
forget their lines . . . Or when his script of earlier days . . .
Must take on new designs . . . The playwright is the genius
who . . . Conceives and who creates . . . The humor, pathos
and suspense . . . And all the players' fates . . . He cannot
guide the actors as . . . They move or smile or sob . . . Because,
at last, that has to be . . . The good director's job . . . He
may not get as much applause . . . As stage celebrities . . .
But he is happy in his fame . . . And with his royalties.

OFFICE WORK

There is no job like office work . . . That seems so hard each
day . . . Nor one that has a lesser chance . . . To bring a raise
in pay . . . So often it appears to be . . . Monotonous routine
. . . And you grow mighty weary of . . . That daily office
scene . . . The same old time each morning and . . . Each
drab, familiar sight . . . The coffee-break, a hurried lunch
. . . And rushing home at night . . . The odds may seem
against you but . . . That really is not true . . . Because the
chance to get ahead . . . Is mainly up to you . . . However
humble is your place . . . Or strong the competition . . .
You have a fair and equal chance . . . To gain your recognition.

HE DID HIS DUTY

What joy is there to quite compare . . . With welcoming
your son . . . When duty is accomplished and . . . His service
days are done? . . . The day we greeted Jimmie as . . . He
left the naval ranks . . . Was one of celebration and . . . Of
everlasting thanks . . . Not just because our boy was home
. . . And he was safe and sound . . . But for those other
blessings we . . . Discovered all around . . . The training
and experience . . . And all he came to know . . . To build
his confidence, and help . . . His character to grow . . . We
thanked our son, who did so well . . . The job he had to do
. . . We thanked almighty God, and thanked . . . The U.S.
Navy, too.

FORGIVE, LET LIVE

Condemn no man for his mistakes . . . However grave they
be . . . Someday you may be asking for . . . A little leniency
. . . For who is he that does not sin . . . Along his earthly
way? . . . Sometimes he falls as frequently . . . As seven times
a day . . . You are no saintly character . . . Among your common brothers . . . If you incline to think that you . . . Are
better than the others . . . Without the helpful grace of God
. . . You could not draw a breath . . . With every passing
second, you . . . Are nearer unto death . . . What profit
can you gain from pride? . . . What fame is yours alone? . . .
Forgive your fellowman his sins . . . As you confess your own.

AS WE ARE ONE

As much as you embrace my heart . . . My heart is happy,
too . . . And every effort I put forth . . . Belongs at last to
you . . . Because whatever day or night . . . Wherever I may
go . . . The more I think of you, my love . . . The more I
love you so . . . The only thing I ask and hope . . . Is that
I may be sure . . . The promise of your faithfulness . . . Will
evermore endure . . . I must be sure that you are mine . . .
As I belong to you . . . That we will live our lives as one . . .
And nevermore as two . . . And with this thought I give you
all . . . The love there is in me . . . To dedicate our future
and . . . Preserve each memory.

BY GOD'S GRACE

The grace of God is all I need . . . To measure my success
. . . Without it I could never hope . . . For health and happi-
ness . . . Without His grace I could not walk . . . Or open up
my eyes . . . To see the beauty of this earth . . . Beneath the
changing skies . . . I could not go to work each day . . . Or
greet the friends I know . . . Unless I had the grace that God
. . . Is willing to bestow . . . And so my life depends on Him
. . . To guide me every day . . . As I obey Him and I live
. . . According to His way . . . And every glory that I gain . . .
While I am on this sod . . . Is one I never could have had . . .
But for the grace of God.

MUSIC IS A DIARY

Music is a diary . . . Of days of long ago . . . The sadness
and the happiness . . . And friends we used to know . . .
When we are young, each song is just . . . Another tune to
sing . . . But as the years go drifting by . . . What memories
they bring! . . . Each melody reminds us of . . . A certain
time and place . . . And on the keyboards of our dreams . . .
We see a special face . . . Yes, music is a diary . . . Of memories to keep . . . Some that we cherish while awake . . . And
others while we sleep . . . Some folks consider music as . . .
Our most important art . . . And they are right because it
keeps . . . A record of the heart.

FAMILY FASHION

Not all the clothes I purchase are . . . My own alone to wear
. . . For some are those that our two sons . . . Are always there
to share . . . The shirts and coats and neckties and . . . Whatever seems to fit . . . Each item is available . . . And they make
use of it . . . Sometimes I wear their articles . . . However old
or new . . . Though these exchanges really are . . . Comparatively few . . . The boys are so much taller that . . . My
slacks would be too short . . . And they could never use my
shoes . . . On street or tennis court . . . But as for kerchiefs,
shirts and ties . . . And dress-up jewelry . . . With both the
boys and Daddy they . . . Are common property.

WHY GET EVEN?

Why do you hunger for revenge . . . When someone hurts
your heart? . . . Why do you keep on hating him . . . Who
played the traitor's part? . . . Where is your sense of kindness and . . . Forgiving attitude? . . . Or do you lock an iron
gate . . . To guard your selfish mood? . . . Perhaps you tell
yourself that you . . . Can even up the score . . . And maybe
you believe that you . . . Deserve a little more . . . But why get
even with your foe? . . . What does it mean to you? . . . When
probably the thing he did . . . He never meant to do? . . . Why
not forgive him and forget . . . And turn the other cheek . . .
As all the earth is promised you . . . If only you are meek?

AS YOU PROPOSE

You ask me now to marry you . . . You ask for my reply . . .
And if I turned you down, my dear . . . Your heart might wonder why . . . Before I answer, let me ask . . . How old are you
today? . . . Not by the number of your years . . . But what you
think and say . . . What are you really looking for? . . . The
moon and stars above? . . . A paradise of happiness . . . In
everlasting love? . . . Or will you keep your faith with me . . .
In sickness and in health . . . And whether we are lucky or
. . . We never live in wealth? . . . If love is really in your
heart . . . Forever deep and true . . . Then be assured, my
darling one . . . I want to marry you.

WE PRAY FOR THEM

We pray, O God, for those who are . . . Our enemies and
Yours . . . That they may change their way of life . . . While
their life still endures . . . Give them, O God, the light to see
. . . The error of their ways . . . That they may kneel before
Your throne . . . And offer You their praise . . . Let not their
evil thoughts prevail . . . Let not their hatred swell . . . And
do not let their ignorance . . . Condemn their souls to hell . . .
We pray for them with all our hearts . . . That they may join
our ranks . . . In honoring and loving You . . . And humbly
saying thanks . . . Forgive them, God—forgive us, too . . .
For all our sins today . . . And give our enemies and Yours . . .
The light to see Your way.

LITTLE FAVOR

The little favor is a thing . . . That we can all afford . . . A simple act of kindness that . . . Does not expect reward . . . It only takes a moment and . . . Of effort, just a bit . . . And God will never fail to bless . . . Our hearts for doing it . . . Of course requests for favors can . . . Become a mountain too . . . Until they are more numerous . . . Than we have time to do . . . But let us serve the best we can . . . By taking them in stride . . . As much as we are able and . . . Our conscience is our guide . . . Each favor is a piece of bread . . . We cast upon the sea . . . That some day will return to kiss . . . Our shore of charity.

GIRL SCOUT KRIS

Kristina is a Girl Scout now . . . And she obeys each rule . . . At home and in the neighborhood . . . And every day in school . . . She used to be a Brownie, and . . . She won a vote of thanks . . . But she has graduated to . . . The happy Girl Scout ranks . . . And now she is a sister true . . . To every Scout she knows . . . And she is fully equal to . . . Each promise they impose . . . Our Kris is good to animals . . . And she is always kind . . . And cheerfulness and thriftiness . . . Are always in her mind . . . But first and most important as . . . A Girl Scout on this sod . . . She knows and does her duty to . . . Her county and to God.

FORGOTTEN FLOWERS?

How often do we go our way . . . And take our friends for
granted . . . Instead of being grateful for . . . The happiness they planted? . . . Instead of giving thanks to them . . .
For all the flowers fair . . . They cultivate so patiently . . .
To show how much they care? . . . The roses of remembrance
for . . . Those moments when we need them . . . The tulips of
advice when we . . . Would be so wise to heed them . . . The
daisies with their sympathy . . . That understand so well . . .
And comfort us in trouble but . . . Our secrets never tell . . .
How often do we praise our friends . . . For all the blessed
hours . . . That are the horticulture of . . . Their fragrant
friendship flowers?

DECIDE MY DREAM

I dream of yesterday and all . . . The life I never had . . .
I dream of one with whom to live . . . And be forever glad
. . . I dream of you, and only you . . . And just to touch your
hand . . . Because somehow I tell myself . . . That you will
understand . . . That you will take my lips to yours . . . In
love and sympathy . . . And with the promise of your heart . . .
You will belong to me . . . But in the vision I behold . . . I
know when it is past . . . The real decision is the one . . .
That you must make at last . . . And as I offer you my love
. . . And give myself to you . . . I hope the verdict you declare
. . . Will make my dream come true.

OBEDIENCE

We owe obedience to God . . . Our flag and family . . . And unto everyone who is . . . In just authority . . . But there obedience does not end . . . Along our earthly way . . . We have to be obedient . . . To all we think and say . . . To be obedient to ourselves . . . By being always true . . . To everything, however small . . . We promise we will do . . . And that is more important now . . . Than any other kind . . . If rightful aims and purposes . . . Are present in the mind . . . Because obedience to ourselves . . . And to each vow we make . . . Is faithfulness to God and flag . . . And for our family's sake.

WHEN CHIPS ARE DOWN

How would you face your troubles, friend . . . If all the chips were down? . . . Would you be strong, or try to play . . . The coward or the clown? . . . You could not laugh them off, you know . . . Nor could you run away . . . Because when all the chips are down . . . It is that final day . . . It is that day of reckoning . . . When every debt is due . . . And if you cannot pay, there is . . . No mercy unto you . . . And so it is in life, as you . . . Are dealing with The Lord . . . And you deserve your punishment . . . Or merit your reward . . . How would you face your Maker now . . . If all the chips were down? . . . With fear of wrath, or faith and hope . . . In your eternal crown?

MY PERFECT ONE

I thought there was no perfect thing . . . Or any perfect one
. . . Or life on earth without a flaw . . . Beneath the moon and
sun . . . Until I saw your loving smile . . . And gazed into
your eyes . . . And in my soul I knew you were . . . As perfect
as the skies . . . As perfect as each little star . . . That twinkles
in the night . . . And every flame that furnishes . . . A steady
candlelight . . . And now I know how good you are . . . How
wonderful to me . . . And how you live for everyone . . . In
all sincerity . . . You may have imperfections as . . . Some
others analyze . . . But, oh, you are and always will . . . Be
perfect in my eyes.

TO DO MY BEST

There are so many things in life . . . I wish that I could do . . .
I know I could not have the time . . . Or strength to see them
through . . . But that is not discouraging . . . Or any reason
why . . . I should not give my best and most . . . Until the day
I die . . . For any part, however small . . . As I pursue my
task . . . If I am persevering, that . . . Is all my God will ask
. . . To do my best from day to day . . . As much as I am able
. . . And what I cannot finish, leave . . . Upon tomorrow's
table . . . For if I do my best today . . . And never steal or bor-
row . . . I know that God will be with me . . . In happiness
and sorrow.

LUXURIOUS FRIEND

Sometimes in life a faithful friend . . . Is a necessity . . . But
in the common course of things . . . He is a luxury . . . He is
that special comfort and . . . Support along our way . . . That
magnifies and multiplies . . . Our happiness each day . . . He
is that extra helping hand . . . So punctual to serve . . . And
frequently more generously . . . Than most of us deserve . . .
Indeed he is a luxury . . . That we could not afford . . . If we
were dutybound to pay . . . His just and full reward . . . So let
us love the friend who stays . . . Through moments bright and
dim . . . And let us always strive to be . . . A replica of him.

MY OWN POOR PRAYER

There are so many written prayers . . . That I could say anew
. . . But now, dear God, I simply want . . . To tell my thoughts
to You . . . I want to whisper from my heart . . . And let You
know myself . . . The troubles and the problems that . . .
Have gathered on my shelf . . . I want to be alone with You
. . . And in my way express . . . The sorrow that I feel for
all . . . The sins that I confess . . . I want to thank You for my
health . . . My small prosperity . . . And every other gift on
earth . . . That You have given me . . . I beg You to forgive
me, God . . . And bless me every day . . . Please listen to this
humble prayer . . . In my imperfect way.

TIMES MUST CHANGE

We think of modern things in life . . . And progress in our day
. . . And make concessions to our youth . . . In all their work
and play . . . We give them greater freedom than . . . Our
childhood ever knew . . . And then we wonder if it is . . . The
proper thing to do . . . We worry for their future as . . . Our
parents were concerned . . . That we might casually forget
. . . The lessons that we learned . . . And yet some changes
must be made . . . As generations pass . . . We cannot freeze
our image in . . . An ancient looking glass . . . But if we do
our best to teach . . . Their hearts to be sincere . . . With honor
unto God and home . . . Then we need never fear.

BRUSH-OFF

I like the brush-off that I get . . . From porter or valet . . . But
not the kind a person gives . . . Who looks and walks away
. . . The shoulder cold that seems to sneer . . . The back
that turns on you . . . The individual who once . . . Pretended
to be true . . . I do not like the character . . . Who poses as a
brother . . . And after having made a date . . . Will break it
for another . . . That brush-off is a cruel thing . . . It shows
a selfish heart . . . It is the point where paths divide . . . And
friends forever part . . . It is unkind, unthinking and . . .
It seems to prove at last . . . The absence of sincerity . . .
Throughout the smiling past.

BACK TO WORK

The holidays are over now . . . The Christmas trees are gone
. . . And as we face our daily task . . . We have to carry on
. . . We have to punch the clock again . . . Each morning
and each night . . . And get sufficient sleep to keep . . . Our
thinking clear and bright . . . And yet we should look happily
. . . Upon that working scene . . . For there is nothing easier
. . . Or smoother than routine . . . We merely do what we
are told . . . And do it every day . . . And at the hour specified
. . . We gather in our pay . . . And as the calendar moves on
. . . Beneath the moon and sun . . . There will be other
holidays . . . To rest and have our fun.

IT MUST BE MEANT

There is no kindness of the heart . . . Or act of charity . . .
If it is selfish or it is . . . Performed reluctantly . . . No favor
we are asked to do . . . Is really worth the while . . . Unless
we instantly comply . . . And do it with a smile . . . For when
we are begrudging as . . . We play the friendly part . . . Quite
obviously our action is . . . Not coming from the heart . . .
It shows that we are insincere . . . And though we pay a price
. . . There is no true affection and . . . There is no sacrifice
. . . So let us think when we are asked . . . For favors great
or small . . . And let us do them willingly . . . Or do them not
at all.

BOUQUET OF LOVE

Each moment I have lived with you . . . Each hour and each
day . . . Has been another flower, dear . . . To freshen our
bouquet . . . Each little whispered word of love . . . Has
been another rose . . . And every kiss a tulip sweet . . . In
poetry or prose . . . The lilacs of our honeymoon . . . The
asters of September . . . Are part of all the fragrant thoughts
. . . We cherish and remember . . . They are the garden of our
love . . . That will forever last . . . Because each flower new becomes . . . A picture of our past . . . And in the vase that holds
them all . . . There is no space today . . . Except as there are
happy blooms . . . To add to our bouquet.

THE HUMAN MIND

The human mind is marvelous . . . As God created it . . . Our
power to approach this life . . . With wisdom and with wit
. . . To make our own decisions as . . . We go along our way
. . . To think whatever thoughts, and choose . . . The words
we want to say . . . To like and love, to scorn and hate . . .
Select our special friends . . . To help or hurt another soul
. . . And strive to make amends . . . The human mind is
actually . . . That freedom of our will . . . Whereby our
promises are those . . . We break or we fulfill . . . But it is only
ours as long . . . As time and tide permit . . . Someday we
must report to God . . . The use we made of it.

I STILL CAN TRY

My sad mistakes are numerous . . . I often wish that I . . .
Could start my life on earth again . . . And never tell a lie
. . . I wish that now I could erase . . . Some words that I have
said . . . In foolish criticism of . . . The living or the dead
. . . I wish I were a child again . . . Without the smallest
fear . . . And God would understand that I . . . Am faithful
and sincere . . . But now there is no turning back . . . I must
go on my way . . . And everything that I have done . . . Belongs to yesterday . . . I cannot change the record but . . . I
can begin anew . . . As God will give me grace for all . . .
The good I want to do.

FINAL FRIEND

A friend is always welcome as . . . The sunshine or a song . . .
But mostly when the tide has turned . . . And everything goes
wrong . . . When castles seem to crumble and . . . Our dreams
would fall apart . . . In desperate moments of regret . . . And
loneliness of heart . . . The friend who still is true to us . . .
However dark our shame . . . Who would not even be the
last . . . To criticize or blame . . . But who would comfort
and console . . . And struggle day and night . . . In every way
in our behalf . . . To help us in our plight . . . Who still is
faithful when it seems . . . Our bridges have been burned . . .
The friend who backs us up when all . . . The other backs are
turned.

ONLY YOU

I would not ever say these words . . . To anyone but you . . .
Because to any other heart . . . My words would not be true
. . . They are the words I whisper, dear . . . To you, and you
alone . . . To tell you that I love you and . . . I want you for
my own . . . You are the only one for me . . . As long as I may
live . . . And only unto you is all . . . The love that I can give
. . . I only hope you will accept . . . The promise of my heart
. . . And give your promise in return . . . That we will never
part . . . There is no other one in life . . . Who means so much
to me . . . Oh, let me take you in my arms . . . For all eternity.

KRISTINA SINGS

Kristina is a pupil now . . . Who wants to learn to sing . . . At
least as lovely as the birds . . . That warble in the spring . . .
Her teacher has informed her that . . . She has a diaphragm
. . . And Krissie tries to breathe and sing . . . By every diagram
. . . She reaches for the higher notes . . . And she is doing good
. . . Without disturbing anyone . . . Around our neighborhood . . . Our daughter does not want to be . . . An operatic
star . . . She only hopes in musicals . . . To measure up to
par . . . And as she minds her teacher, and . . . She follows
every word . . . We feel someday her voice will be . . .
Appreciatively heard.

WHO HAVE NO HOME

I like to travel everywhere . . . And take in all the sights . . .
With happy friendships old and new . . . To fill the days and
nights . . . But sometimes I am gone too long . . . And then the
hours drag . . . While emptiness surrounds my room . . . And
laughter seems to lag . . . I miss my children and my wife . . .
Who are so dear to me . . . And I am lonesome for the love
. . . Of my dear family . . . And yet as I remember them . . .
Wherever I may roam . . . I think of those who have no place
. . . That they may call a home . . . I think of those who live
alone . . . Who hunger and who yearn . . . Who travel and
who have no one . . . To whom they may return.

VALENTINE PRAYER

I say a prayer of gratitude . . . That you are really mine . . .
And may God always bless your soul . . . My loving valentine
. . . God bless you for your faithfulness . . . And kindliness to
me . . . And all the joy that I have known . . . In your sweet
company . . . There is no other heart alive . . . As bountiful
as yours . . . Or one in which the warmth of love . . . So
ardently endures . . . You are my precious valentine . . . In
every happy way . . . Not once a year but all around . . . The
clock of every day . . . And so I say this grateful prayer . . .
May God be good to you . . . And may my humble efforts
help . . . To make your dreams come true.

TRUE COMPANIONSHIP

Whatever happiness in life . . . Of mind or heart or lip . . .
There is no joy that can compare . . . With true companionship
. . . The true companionship that brings . . . The mind and
heart together . . . And speaks in whispers that are heard
. . . Above the loudest weather . . . It is that understanding
bond . . . Of love and sympathy . . . Much more than just the
friendliness . . . Of being neighborly . . . The willingness to
sacrifice . . . Beyond the call of duty . . . In order to preserve
and share . . . This life in all its beauty . . . The true companionship is one . . . That tips the human scales . . . As one
sincerely tries, and not . . . If he succeeds or fails.

I STILL BELIEVE

When I was just a little child . . . I thought the world was
mine . . . That everything was beautiful . . . And everyone
benign . . . That life on earth was wonderful . . . With everybody good . . . And peace and joy a natural part . . . Of every
neighborhood . . . And then I learned that there was sin . . .
And people who did wrong . . . And never any life on earth
. . . Could be a perfect song . . . And so I found eventually
. . . That I was human too . . . And I must face temptation's
war . . . As others have to do . . . It was a disappointment
but . . . I am much older now . . . And by the grace of God
I still . . . May keep my every vow.

SO MUCH IN LOVE

I am so much in love with you . . . I know not what to say
. . . Except that you are wonderful . . . You take my breath
away . . . My mind gets dizzy, and my heart . . . Is bound to
skip a beat . . . Each time we share the telephone . . . And
every time we meet . . . I only have to look at you . . . Or listen
to your voice . . . And I am really positive . . . I want no other
choice . . . You are the only one for me . . . As long as I may
live . . . The one I love and long to serve . . . With all that
I can give . . . There is no other one on earth . . . For whom
my soul could yearn . . . I love you and I beg of you . . . To
love me in return.

FAMILY PRAYER

We come to You, O Lord and God . . . We pray on bended
knee . . . For Your eternal blessing to . . . Enfold our family
. . . That You will bless us always but . . . Especially today
. . . With all the graces that we need . . . To help us on our
way . . . Forgive us for our failures and . . . Our errors of the
past . . . And for our lack of courage when . . . The sky
was overcast . . . Give us the strength to follow You . . . And
always to obey . . . In every thought and word and deed . . .
According to Your way . . . However great our fortune or . . .
Whatever tragedy . . . We want to serve You as a true . . . And
loving family.

THE PARK

The park is such a peaceful place . . . To pause and meditate
. . . From early dawn until the dusk . . . And through the
hours late . . . Where one may walk in loneliness . . . Yet
never be alone . . . For there are children in the park . . .
And people who are grown . . . And there are trees and flowers
or . . . The snows of yesterday . . . With shadows in the moonlight of . . . A dream that passed away . . . However loud the
voices near . . . A silence fills the mind . . . As tragedy and
bitterness . . . Are fading far behind . . . There is a stillness on
the ground . . . A freshness in the air . . . And in one's soul
the faith renewed . . . That God is everywhere.

PUBLIC RELATIONS

In business, profession . . . Or dealing with nations . . . Of
vital importance . . . Are public relations . . . They are the
relations not really related . . . As brothers and sisters . . .
Or those who have mated . . . But they are the envoys . . . Of
careful expression . . . That lead to a triumph . . . Or gain a
concession . . . Our public relations . . . Can make us or break
us . . . With friends who admire . . . Or those who forsake us
. . . They are the top salesmen . . . In all of our dealings . . .
As much as we comfort . . . Or injure some feelings . . . So
let us be mindful . . . Of public relations . . . And let us be
tactful . . . With plenty of patience.

BY ANY FIGURE

I list my days of happiness . . . I count my dreams come true
. . . And when I total them, my love . . . They all add up to
you . . . And then they multiply themselves . . . With every
passing minute . . . As often as I have a thought . . . And you
are always in it . . . But there is no division, dear . . . Except
as we divide . . . Our smiles and tears throughout the years
. . . As we go side by side . . . And as I face each problem
now . . . There can be no subtraction . . . My love would never
lessen by . . . The very smallest fraction . . . You are my math,
my algebra . . . The one that I adore . . . And even in geometry
. . . I could not love you more.

UNSPOILED

All children who are spoiled are not . . . The ones whose folks
are rich . . . They may belong to families . . . That have to save
each stitch . . . The spoiling of a child is not . . . A case of
ready money . . . Or lavishing affection that . . . Is sweeter
than all honey . . . Invariably it comes about . . . Through
giving them their way . . . Without the good example that
. . . They need from day to day . . . Some boys and girls re-
mained unspoiled . . . Because they have the breeding . . .
To understand the compromise . . . Required in succeeding
. . . They follow the example of . . . Their mother and their
dad . . . With thanks for opportunities . . . They never might
have had.

IN YOUR HANDS

You asked me for my promise and . . . I promise you today . . .
That I will always be your own . . . In every loving way
. . . That I will keep and comfort you . . . However dark the
night . . . However many storms may be . . . To fill your heart
with fright . . . Yes, I will take you to my breast . . . And hold
you in my arms . . . And I will cherish you, my dear . . . And
all your golden charms . . . And even if you change your mind
. . . My heart will still be true . . . Because there is no other
one . . . Who can compare with you . . . So now you know I
am your own . . . Forever and a day . . . And whether you and
I shall wed . . . Is up to you to say.

DESERVING WIFE

Sometimes I wonder if I am . . . Of any earthly use . . . Considering how I endure . . . The storm and the abuse . . . Of
course I am referring to . . . My daily family life . . . And more
especially to her . . . Who is my loving wife . . . If anything
goes wrong at home . . . I have to take the blame . . . But just
my smallest door-prize is . . . A credit to her name . . . And if
I am promoted and . . . I get a raise in pay . . . She claims she is
responsible . . . That I am on my way . . . And yet whatever
praise is mine . . . Whoever may have said it . . . I must confess
that, after all . . . She does deserve the credit.

HE WORKED HIS WAY

The person who is truly great . . . Is humble as can be . . .
And usually his rise to fame . . . Began in poverty . . . And
usually he struggled with . . . His daily sweat and tears . . .
A thousand sacrifices in . . . The bloom of youthful years . . .
But when his name is recognized . . . So few appreciate . . .
The credit he deserves and which . . . Is just a little late
. . . They think he always "had it" and . . . He is a lucky
guy . . . And everything he touches is . . . Another golden sky
. . . Success is not in terms of cash . . . Or influence on earth
. . . But only as the struggling heart . . . Can prove its greater
worth.

BE GOOD TO THEM

If now my life is over, God . . . And I have reached my end
. . . I ask Your mercy, not for me . . . But for my every
friend . . . I know it is too late for me . . . To make amends
to You . . . For everything that I did wrong . . . Or that I
failed to do . . . Dear God, be good to all my friends . . . Who
have been good to me . . . Give them at least a corner small
. . . In Your eternity . . . They have been faithful unto me
. . . Until my time to die . . . And in their charity have lived
. . . A better life than I . . . Be good to all who have been
kind . . . To any small extent . . . And let me suffer for my
sins . . . Whatever punishment.

CAST PARTY

Beyond the final curtain, where . . . A play is in the past . . .
There is that gay occasion of . . . A party for the cast . . .
When actresses and actors and . . . Production staff and all
. . . Relax in celebration of . . . The labors they recall . . .
The hours of rehearsals and . . . The tension everywhere . . .
When finally and fearfully . . . That opening night was there
. . . It is the special party where . . . They joke and "ham"
their parts . . . And they exchange those compliments . . .
Sincerely from their hearts . . . And hope that they will meet
again . . . Before the footlights bright . . . With like applause
or even more . . . Than they received tonight.

I KNOW IN MY HEART

I know that when the years are gone . . . And we are old and
gray . . . I shall adore you just as much . . . As I love you today . . . Because I feel it in my heart . . . And even in the air
. . . That you will always be the one . . . For whom I really
care . . . The storms may come, the trees may fall . . . The
bombs burst all about . . . The last small candle flicker and
. . . The final flame go out . . . But there will always be the
glow . . . Of my deep love for you . . . And when the last
lie has been told . . . My heart will still be true . . . I shall
belong to you, my love . . . Whatever else may be . . . Beyond
the darkest night and then . . . For all eternity.

Every month belongs to God . . . The same as every day . . .
But there is added cause for joy . . . When Sunday opens May
. . . For Sunday is the special time . . . We honor Him each
week . . . Adore Him and implore Him for . . . The favors
that we seek . . . And May is something special on . . . Our
calendar each year . . . Because it is that merry month . . .
For all His children dear . . . The children that belong to God
. . . Who placed them in our care . . . And Who bestows
His blessings great . . . On parents everywhere . . . And so
as May and Sunday blend . . . To shape this special morn
. . . Let us adore and thank Him for . . . Each baby that is
born.

MORTGAGE

The mortgage is a helping hand . . . A ladder to success . . .
It is a chain of stepping stones . . . To peace and happiness
. . . Provided you can step on each . . . And go along your
way . . . With confidence each month in your . . . Ability to
pay . . . It is your chance to buy a home . . . Or start a busi-
ness new . . . With cash you need but which as yet . . . Has
not been earned by you . . . The mortage is your honor badge
. . . In town and neighborhood . . . Because it truly signifies
. . . Your credit must be good . . . Yet never any sugar can . . .
Be sweeter in a cup . . . As that old mortgage on the day . . .
When you can burn it up.

TO GET ALONG

Your neighbors and their friendship may . . . Be like a perfect song . . . Or they may be the ones with whom . . . You do not get along . . . They may be jealous of your wealth . . . Or snub your poverty . . . Or they may want to share this life . . . And help your family . . . Perhaps they have a dog or cat . . . That gets into your way . . . Or you have little children who . . . Annoy them when they play . . . These are the common problems of . . . The average neighborhood . . . And for each side it must be said . . . There is some bad and good . . . There has to be a compromise . . . For folks to get along . . . As only in companionship . . . Is any perfect song.

I PROMISE MY HEART

I love you for your charming self . . . The way you smile at me . . . And for the humble creature that . . . You always try to be . . . I love you for your constant heart . . . Your certain faith in God . . . And for your willingness to share . . . Our life upon this sod . . . I could not match your goodness, but . . . I promise I will strive . . . To bring you every happiness . . . And keep our love alive . . . I promise I will cherish you . . . From every rising sun . . . Until each dark or starry night . . . Declares the day is done . . . I love you and I want you, dear . . . As long as I may live . . . With all the heartfelt gratitude . . . That I could ever give.

THE NAME OF MOTHER

The mother who deserves that name . . . Is one whose child comes first . . . In comfort and in happiness . . . In hunger and in thirst . . . The little boy or little girl . . . To whom her womb gave birth . . . And who means more to her than does . . . Her life upon this earth . . . She is the mother who is good . . . Unselfish and afraid . . . Who does not wander off and leave . . . Her children to a maid . . . She does not think about herself . . . The jewels she might wear . . . But only that her boy or girl . . . Will get the best of care . . . There are a million mothers but . . . They are not all the same . . . And only she who loves her child . . . Deserves that noble name.

TO LIVE FOR HIM

What does it matter if I live . . . Tomorrow or today . . . Unless my heart and soul can help . . . In some important way? . . . Unless I lead my neighbor to . . . His glory in the sun . . . And show him all the goodness that . . . His charity has won? . . . Unless I share the sky with him . . . And every kind of weather . . . And be his faithful friend as long . . . As we can be together? . . . Whatever course I take in life . . . However I may end . . . I want to keep him in my heart . . . Forever as a friend . . . So let me live for him as long . . . As I am on this sod . . . For as I serve my neighbor I . . . Am faithful unto God.

DO YOU READ GOD?

Have you a Bible in your home? . . . Is reading it a "must"?
. . . Do you peruse it now and then . . . Or does it gather
dust? . . . How often do you pick it up . . . And turn another
page? . . . How much are you concerned about . . . The
sacredness of age? . . . The sacredness of wisdom that . . .
Is handed down the years . . . The wisdom of the prophets that
. . . Has told our smiles and tears . . . The Bible is The Word
of God . . . As He would have us know . . . The teachings we
must follow and . . . The row we have to hoe . . . How often
do you think of it . . . Or even take a look . . . To read the holy
words that are . . . Our most important book?

FOR YOUR CHRISTMAS

With all my heart I cherish you . . . With all my love I say
. . . I wish a world of happiness . . . For you on Christmas
Day . . . I hope the morning will be bright . . . And all the
heavens blue . . . And on this birthday of His Son . . . God
will be good to you . . . I pray that you will never know . . .
The very smallest tear . . . Unless it be a drop of joy . . . To
hold forever dear . . . Because you are so wonderful . . . And,
oh, it means so much . . . To hear your soothing voice or just
. . . To feel your gentle touch . . . I wish and say, I hope and
pray . . . This Christmas Day will be . . . The perfect one
for you because . . . You are so good to me.

THE PEACEFUL LIFE

The simple, ordinary life . . . With struggles every day . . .
Is happier than luxury . . . Along an easy way . . . Of course
it may not seem to be . . . And we may envy those . . . Who
ride in gorgeous cars and wear . . . The most expensive
clothes . . . But as we share our work and play . . . And strive
to do some good . . . We gain the love and friendship of . . .
Our humble neighborhood . . . We gather all the wealth on
earth . . . That money cannot buy . . . The smile sincere, the
honest tear . . . And every heartfelt sigh . . . And, most of
all, the peace of mind . . . In doing what is right . . . That
lets our conscience slumber when . . . We go to bed at night.

MY LONELY MOMENTS

My only lonely moments are . . . The ones away from you . . .
And only in those moments, dear . . . I know not what to do
. . . I need the love and comfort that . . . You constantly bestow . . . They are my faith and courage and . . . The only
hope I know . . . I need you every moment from . . . The
rising of the sun . . . Until its rays are vanished and . . . Another day is done . . . And then I need you in my dreams . . .
From darkness unto dawn . . . And I am lonely in my heart
. . . Whenever you are gone . . . The only moments of our
years . . . When I have ever cried . . . Have been those lonely
moments when . . . You were not at my side.

BLESS MY FRIENDS

I ask You, God, to help my friends . . . Wherever they may be . . . As much as all of them have been . . . Considerate to me . . . As much as they have helped me in . . . My moments of despair . . . And put a crutch beneath my arm . . . To help me climb the stair . . . Give them Your special blessing, God . . . Each hour of the day . . . And when they travel anywhere . . . Protect them on their way . . . I have so many weaknessess . . . There is so much I lack . . . That in a thousand years from now . . . I could not pay them back . . . Give them the shelter that they need . . . The clothes and drink and food . . . In answer to my prayer to You . . . Of love and gratitude.

BRIEF CASE

The brief case is the travel case . . . Of your portfolio . . . That keeps your business at your side . . . Wherever you may go . . . Those all-important memos of . . . Instruction from your boss . . . Including recent statements cold . . . Of profit and of loss . . . Of course it also has some room . . . For personal affairs . . . The letters and the snapshots gay . . . And all your family cares . . . And sometimes it is large enough . . . To hold a shirt and tie . . . And other small necessities . . . You need to "just get by" . . . The brief case can be cumbersome . . . But sometimes it is light . . . It all depends on whether you . . . Are doing what is right.

Our children always were so good . . . About this time of year
. . . Because they knew that Christmas Day . . . Was draw-
ing very near . . . And they are just as good today . . . As in
that golden past . . . But childhood is the parents' joy . . . That
cannot ever last . . . Our boys are both in college now . . .
And sister is so tall . . . That being good for Santa Claus . . .
Is no concern at all . . . Yes, they are good but, oh, we wish
. . . We had a little shaver . . . Who just about this time of
year . . . Would be on best behavior . . . Of course, we have no
reason now . . . To worry or to fuss . . . We simply have to wait
until . . . A grandchild comes to us.

INDEBTED TO YOU

I am indebted to you, dear . . . Beyond my life to pay . . . For
all your love and comfort and . . . Your kindness every day
. . . For your encouragement and faith . . . Your thoughtful-
ness of me . . . And in my moments of distress . . . Your loyal
sympathy . . . I could not ever pay you back . . . In dollars
or in dimes . . . In diamonds or emeralds . . . Or worlds of
happy times . . . But this much I can promise, dear . . . My
heart belongs to you . . . And you are in my every thought
. . . And everything I do . . . And always I will go to you
. . . At every beck and call . . . Prepared to serve your slightest
wish . . . And give my very all.

THE ADE THAT AIDS

An orangeade or lemonade . . . Is just another drink . . . And
yet it is the beverage . . . That makes a person think . . . It is
not just the cooling quaff . . . That quenches summer thirst
. . . Or something on the children's list . . . That they consider first . . . An ade is real American . . . And it is quite an
aid . . . For every youth in school or sports . . . To make a
higher grade . . . And it is filled with memories . . . For older
folks today . . . The single glass, the pair of straws . . . That
sipped their hearts away . . . Whatever flavor it may hold . . .
The cherry, grape or lime . . . The ade is still delicious and
. . . Important in our time.

KRISTINA'S TROPHY

Kristina was so happy when . . . She won a statue small . . .
And reasonably proud that she . . . Had won out over all . . .
She had a perfect right to smile . . . Upon her recognition . . .
For she was really up against . . . The toughest competition
. . . The contest was in drama and . . . She was but thirteen
years . . . With not too much experience . . . And all her
girlish fears . . . But, oh, that trophy meant so much . . . It
always will inspire . . . Our daughter to continue her . . .
Theatrical desire . . . And though Kristina still may be . . .
Of somewhat tender age . . . We feel that she is headed for
. . . Success upon the stage.

FAITHFUL HEART

My friends are quite as numerous . . . As are the stars above
. . . But just a few of them are in . . . The circle of my love
. . . They are the ones who keep in touch . . . And mean the
words they say . . . Instead of merely drifting with . . . The
weather of the day . . . Instead of disappearing when . . . My
progress seems too light . . . And when my prospects for success
. . . Are not exactly bright . . . The others do not matter and
. . . Although I say hello . . . They are the ones I chance to
meet . . . But do not really know . . . The circle of my friends
is formed . . . By what they say and do . . . As only in the faithful heart . . . Is any friendship true.

LET US REPEAT

Let me repeat myself, my dear . . . That I am yours today
. . . And that my heart belongs to you . . . In every loving
way . . . Let me repeat the vows I made . . . When we stood
side by side . . . There, in the presence of our God . . . The
bridegroom and the bride . . . Do you remember what it meant
. . . When all was said and done . . . And as we spoke those
sacred words . . . We two became as one? . . . Let me repeat
that history . . . And so remind you too . . . I gave you everything in life . . . I had to offer you . . . So let me hear your
heart repeat . . . The words you said to me . . . As I would
hold and treasure you . . . For all eternity.

I HOPE THIS SPRING

The sun is warm upon the earth . . . I hear the robin sing
. . . And in my eager heart I know . . . That it is almost
spring . . . And in my heart I also know . . . I love you more
and more . . . And all my thoughts are messengers . . . Who
knock upon your door . . . Each flower in my garden is . . .
A fragrant wish for you . . . And every prayer I say is one
. . . That God will bless us two . . . That springtime is our season and . . . That this will be the year . . . When you and I
become as one . . . By every vow sincere . . . I hope this is our
wondrous spring . . . With many more ahead . . . As we
embrace each other and . . . Divide our daily bread.

FRAGILE FRIENDSHIP

Friendship is a fragile thing . . . However strong it seems . . .
So many times a single word . . . Can shatter all our dreams
. . . It is so easy to offend . . . Or to misunderstand . . . Because our feelings are so hard . . . To conquer and command
. . . It is a human frailty . . . To lack the common sense . . .
Of overlooking certain deeds . . . That mean no real offense
. . . And now and then we utter thoughts . . . That we did not
intend . . . To criticize or ever hurt . . . The feelings of a
friend . . . And so the strength of friendship is . . . Our tolerance at last . . . As we forgive each other and . . . Forget
about the past.

WHO LIVE TO EAT

Some people merely live to eat . . . Some people seem to thrive
. . . On many times the calories . . . They need to stay alive
. . . But do they really thrive at last? . . . How comfortable
are they? . . . And what is their expectancy . . . To live another day? . . . They may enjoy three solid meals . . . And
something on the sly . . . A little leg of chicken or . . . Another piece of pie . . . But how about that overweight? . . .
That pressure of the blood? . . . Or nervous ulcers that result
. . . From gulping down the cud? . . . Why do some people
live to eat . . . Who have so much to give . . . When they
could help the whole wide world . . . If they would eat to live?

I OWE YOU SO MUCH

You have been just as good and kind . . . As anyone could be
. . . And, more than anybody else . . . You have encouraged
me . . . You have provided faith and hope . . . In hours that
were dark . . . And urged me on, if only by . . . Your whisper
in the park . . . You have inspired me to fight . . . No matter
what the cost . . . And moved my spirit when I thought . . .
That everything was lost . . . What more could you have done
for me . . . Than just to help me thrive? . . . Indeed without
your faith in me . . . I would not be alive . . . I love you and
I thank you and . . . I hope what good I do . . . Will be a small
down-payment, dear . . . On all I owe to you.

NO FANTASY

My God is not a fantasy . . . He is no superstition . . . He is
the Bible and He is . . . My human intuition . . . He is my
Lord and Master as . . . My pastor teaches me . . . But also
God is obvious . . . In everything I see . . . The changing seasons of the year . . . With every kind of weather . . . The
universe of sun and moon . . . And stars that shine together
. . . And He is all the miracles . . . That stay the hand of death
. . . To keep an old man on his feet . . . Or save a baby's
breath . . . I know my God as I am taught . . . To face all tears
and laughter . . . And I must serve Him on this earth . . . To
be with Him hereafter.

OUR STATION WAGON

Vacation trips are wonderful . . . With all the sights there
are . . . Especially for the family . . . That has a brand new
car . . . And that is why we're happy with . . . Our station
wagon new . . . As we prepare to travel and . . . To take in
every view . . . This is our first experience . . . In station
wagon style . . . And all the indications are . . . That it will
be worth while . . . There's so much room for luggage and . . .
To stretch and rest our feet . . . And all of the upholstery
. . . Is beautiful and neat . . . And there is lots of extra space
. . . For relatives and friends . . . Who want to share our
junkets or . . . To visit on weekends.

WHY DISCOURAGED?

Why do we get discouraged as . . . We go along our way . . .
When life is just a calendar . . . That moves from day to day?
. . . Each morning is about the same . . . As that which came
before . . . With disappointments and with joys . . . That
knock upon our door . . . We laugh and cry, and we are fraught
. . . With confidence and fear . . . And there is little difference
. . . From week to month and year . . . Our problems are the
same today . . . As they have always been . . . And if we fail,
another chance . . . Is still our own to win . . . Why should we
be discouraged in . . . The darkness where we grope . . . As
long as we believe in God . . . And have eternal hope?

ALL THAT YOU WANT

Dear one, if there is anything . . . That I can do for you . . .
Please tell me your desires, and . . . Your wishes will come
true . . . If now you search for comfort in . . . Some darkness
where you grope . . . If you need great encouragement . . .
Or just a ray of hope . . . Or if your heart is happy but . . .
You want it to be more . . . With golden opportunities . . . To
knock upon your door . . . You may be sure that all my strength
. . . Of body and of mind . . . Will be at your disposal for
. . . Whatever you would find . . . I need not tell you why, my
dear . . . For you already know . . . That I would give my
life for you . . . Because I love you so.

HER PARENTS

I do not like the "in-law" term . . . Anent the marriage state
. . . Because it has become a form . . . Of comedy or hate . . .
I never speak of "in-laws" to . . . My wife or anyone . . .
Her parents are my parents, and . . . I want to be their son
. . . What cause is there for ridicule . . . Or animosity . . .
Because two households now become . . . A single family?
. . . We may not get along at first . . . But that is no excuse
. . . For treating "in-law" relatives . . . With laughter or
abuse . . . In all our years of marriage there . . . Has been no
family strife . . . Her parents are not "in-laws" but . . . The
parents of my wife.

I MEAN IT, DEAR

The moments I have had with you . . . I never could repent
. . . For they have been the happiest . . . That I have ever
spent . . . Inside your heart there may be doubt . . . That what
I said is true . . . "There is no other one on earth . . . Who can
compare with you" . . . But, darling, please believe me, as
. . . I say those words again . . . For they are just as sacred
now . . . As any promise then . . . And, oh, I want you every
day . . . To love and hold and keep . . . Each morning we
awake and rise . . . Each night we go to sleep . . . I would
not trifle with your heart . . . My soul is too sincere . . . Myself and all my worldly goods . . . I offer you, my dear.

BONUS

The bonus is a special sum . . . The boss presents to you . . .
For having done a better job . . . Than you were asked to do
. . . It is not just a cash reward . . . For some achievement
great . . . Or an incentive to the ones . . . Who ought to
concentrate . . . It is an honor medal and . . . A mark of
business beauty . . . Above required labor and . . . Beyond the
call of duty . . . The bonus real is not a gift . . . In any business
sense . . . Nor is it meant to compensate . . . For self-incurred
expense . . . It is the exclamation mark . . . That punctuates
the praise . . . When your superiors are pleased . . . With your
successful ways.

TO SERVE YOU, GOD

I am Your smallest creature, God . . . Your softest and Your
least . . . I am no leader on this earth . . . No president or priest
. . . I set no great example for . . . The world to follow me . . .
I simply try to live Your way . . . In all humility . . . I do not
search for any praise . . . Or glory on this sod . . . I only want
to do Your will . . . And worship You, my God . . . To love my
neighbor as myself . . . And do my daily deed . . . For every
relative and friend . . . And everyone in need . . . Please give
me grace and strength to live . . . Whatever days remain . . .
As I would be Your servant, God . . . In sunshine and in rain.